K What Teachers Should
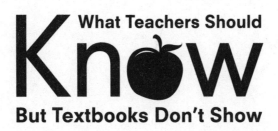
n w
But Textbooks Don't Show

This book is dedicated to my grandmother, Harmony,
whose wisdom and spirit have sustained me in my
classroom and throughout my life.

What Teachers Should Know But Textbooks Don't Show

STELLA ERBES

Skyhorse Publishing

Skyhorse Publishing books may be purchased in bulk at special discounts for sales promotion, corporate gifts, fund-raising, or educational purposes. Special editions can also be created to specifications. For details, contact the Special Sales Department, Sky Pony Press, 307 West 36th Street, 11th Floor, New York, NY 10018 or info@skyhorsepublishing.com.

Skyhorse® and Skyhorse Publishing® are registered trademark of Skyhorse Publishing, Inc.®, a Delaware corporation.

Visit our website at www.skyhorsepublishing.com.

10 9 8 7 6 5 4 3 2 1

Library of Congress Cataloging-in-Publication Data is available on file.

Cover design by Scott Van Atta

Print ISBN: 978-1-63450-724-0
Ebook ISBN: 978-1-63450-727-1

Printed in the United States of America

Contents

Acknowledgments

I am grateful to the many people who have stood alongside me during the different phases of this book. I acknowledge that this book could not have been completed without the key people whom I have had the good fortune to have met along the path of this journey, and those who have been my continual support system and have never faltered in supporting, encouraging, loving, and blessing me.

I will be forever grateful to Jean Ward for recognizing my passion, embracing my enthusiasm, and opening the door that led to this book. To all the key team players at Corwin Press—Hudson, Jenn, Ed, and Scott—thank you for your professionalism, your fine editing skills, your creative talents, and for investing in me and my dreams to share my enthusiasm, love, and knowledge of teaching with others.

To my mom and dad, I thank you for being my examples of courage and perseverance, and for working so hard all your lives to give me a life full of abundant opportunities. To my big brother John and my beautiful sister-in-law Arlene, you both inspire me to believe in myself and to work hard so that all my dreams may come true. Because of you, I know there are no limits to what I can accomplish.

To my amazing husband, Richard, and my precious sons, Josh and Jacob—thank you for giving me the time and space to complete my first book, for being proud of me, and for always believing in me no matter what I do.

To my families at Moorpark High School, Peach Hill Academy, Oaks Christian School, and Pepperdine University—from these places I have learned the finest pearls of wisdom in teaching and experienced my most valuable memories as a teacher. I have been blessed to have worked alongside great teachers, administrators, staff members, and students. Thanks to all of you for allowing me to share all the helpful lessons that I learned from or with you in this book.

To those who read countless rough drafts and cheered me on throughout the entire writing process—Ann, April, Carol, Damian, my "sistah" Donna, Erin, Kendra, Marilyn, Melodee, and Nicky, I know this book is more improved and polished because you were all a part of it.

To special angels like the Rasmussens for sharing their home in Balboa as a quiet haven for me to retreat to so that I could complete my writing, and to other serendipitous friends whom I met along this journey and were there to toast to chapters completed and milestones reached, I thank you for your support.

It is with great pride and honor that I acknowledge these key people who have helped me to pour my heart, mind, spirit, and soul into each chapter of this book, and it is to them that I give thanks.

Stephanie van Hover
Assistant Professor
Curry School of Education, University of Virginia
Charlottesville, VA

Jennifer W. Ramamoorthi
PDS Site Coordinator, Illinois State University
Community Consolidated School District 21
Wheeling, IL

About the Author

 **Stella Erbes** earned her PhD in educational psychology and master's degrees in education and Spanish from the University of California, Santa Barbara. Her 16 years of teaching experiences span both the elementary and secondary levels as well as the public, private, and homeschooling sectors. Currently, she is an Assistant Professor of Teacher Education at Pepperdine University, where she teaches courses in educational psychology and secondary teaching methods, and supervises student teachers. Although she enjoyed teaching in the K–12 classroom, Stella decided to begin a career in teacher education in 2002 so that she could support beginning teachers as they entered the world of teaching by sharing practical knowledge gained from her wide array of experiences. Stella's research interests focus on beginning teacher support, teaching methodologies, and undergraduate research experiences. Her research has been presented at internationally recognized conferences such as the annual meeting of the American Educational Research Association. It is her hope that teachers in K–12 classrooms and researchers in higher education can partner more closely to connect theory and practice in valuable ways so that both classroom teachers and university professors can be well informed of current issues and trends in today's schools. Stella resides in Moorpark, California, with her husband Richard and two school-age sons, Joshua and Jacob.

Introduction

I t is extremely difficult to describe to beginning teachers what their first year of teaching will be like—the planning, the paperwork, the parents, and the pressure. Although new teachers have completed full-time student teaching, this is a sheltered form of reality. Until they assume responsibility for their own classrooms, new teachers will not have a true understanding of all the challenges that teaching presents. However, after surviving the hurdles of the first year, there is a great sense of accomplishment, honor, and reward, and each year thereafter gets better.

For a new teacher, the first stage is one of survival and a desperate search for the tools needed to move past this phase. Although beginning teacher support programs are being implemented now more than ever, it is still common to encounter new teachers who feel overwhelmed as they are faced with the challenges of gathering resources for their daily lessons, managing the clerical and clinical sides of teaching, and seeking a way to balance their personal and professional lives. As a beginner, I did not have a systematic form of support or a teaching mentor who was officially assigned to me and could orient me to simple clerical tasks, school culture, or the bureaucracy of education. Instead, I reflected back upon my preparation and scoured through my education textbooks searching for helpful tips that might aid me to deal better with the shock of assuming the responsibilities of my own classroom. Unfortunately, I found little or no information in these sources about practical insights into the world of teaching.

The main focus of education textbooks and classes is to transmit the differing philosophies of teaching and lesson planning. Information that bridges the gap between educational theory and actual classroom practice is lacking. New teachers search for the practical knowledge that the veterans of their profession possess;

these are the critical bits of information that can be achieved only through experience. This insider knowledge, coupled with the historical and valuable research of teaching, is the missing link that new teachers seek and may be what is needed to make the transition into the teaching profession smoother for beginning teachers. However, given that teachers spend most of their time in classrooms separated from their colleagues, the likelihood of veteran teachers having the opportunity to share this hidden curriculum with new teachers is minimal. As a result, this vital, practical knowledge continues to be missing for those entering our profession, and many new teachers continue to suffer through the survival stage just as I did.

More efforts have been made to help beginning teachers with the inception of new teacher mentor programs and beginning teacher support programs. However, beginning teachers have criticized these mechanisms of support for repeating the topics of standards-based instruction and professional development already covered in their teacher preparation programs. For example, aligning lesson plans with state standards and formulating professional goals to develop as an educator are key topics that beginning teacher support programs typically address. Although these dimensions of teaching are important, new teachers are hungry for the insider's knowledge of teaching that experienced teachers possess. Beginning teachers seek the valuable lessons learned through practical experience. More specifically, new teachers are interested in learning how veteran teachers might answer the following questions:

- How do I run the first day of class?
- How do I manage my time effectively?
- How do I get all the grading or preparation done?
- How do I manage, discipline, and teach my students successfully?
- How do I get the students to respect me and to like me?
- How do I make learning fun in my classroom if I am not particularly creative?

These practical insights into the world of teaching appeared to be missing from my college textbooks and are not commonly found in a clear, concise, and friendly text for teachers, whether new or experienced. The stories, tips, and useful knowledge that teachers learn while on the job need to be disseminated and shared within our profession, for these are the gems of information that help all teachers thrive.

Having worked in K–12 education for 10 years and now working in teacher education at the university level, I serve as the veteran teacher or mentor to many prospective teachers each semester. When asked the question, "Do you think I should be a teacher?" my thoughts and memories are filled with joy, enthusiasm, passion, and a bit of concern as I try to describe to the students how much work is involved in teaching, especially in the early years. Then I always encourage the students by explaining that teaching will change their lives. And for me, now 16 years after joining the teaching profession, I look back on my own experiences and know that I have never regretted my decision to answer the calling to be a teacher.

In reflecting on my own journey as a teacher, I wished that I had more opportunities to glean valuable and insightful lessons from experienced teachers. It is easy to become so involved in our own cultures that we overlook the little nuances that would be helpful to newcomers and are essential to surviving and thriving in that culture. This, combined with the limited interactions of teachers in schools, makes it difficult for such information to be shared. It is my hope that with this book, all teachers will benefit from some personal, simple, and valuable lessons and insights that were learned the hard way by me and other new teachers and that have helped the beginning teachers whom I have mentored to make faster and easier transitions into this noble field.

The beauty of these lessons learned from teaching is that they are not simply lessons for teachers—rather, in my student teaching classes, I refer to them as "life lessons" and believe that they can be adapted to other workplaces, mentor programs, and even to parenting. Although teaching poses many challenges, it can be more rewarding than simple words can describe. Many of my own triumphs and successes in teaching can be attributed to the practical knowledge and insights into teaching that colleagues and friends have shared with me. And so, as you, too, embark upon or continue the journey of being a teacher, I hope that you will be able to use these practical insights into the world of teaching to empower and inspire you to take the actions necessary to transition successfully into this profession and thrive in it for years to come.

PART I

Planning and Preparing to Teach

CHAPTER ONE

Making Positive First Impressions

An understanding heart is everything in a teacher, and cannot be esteemed highly enough. One looks back with appreciation to the brilliant teachers, but with gratitude to those who touched our human feeling. The curriculum is so much necessary raw material, but warmth is the vital element for the growing plant and for the soul of the child.

—Carl Jung

The first day of school is an exciting and anxious time for everyone and sets the stage for a multitude of first impressions. During this time, both students and parents formulate their initial impressions of teachers and their classes. In the same way, teachers informally begin to assess the personalities, minds, and cultural backgrounds of the many students whom they have been paired with for the academic year. All of these initial judgments can potentially influence a student's sense of self-efficacy and overall achievement in school. Personal interactions between students, as well as those between students and teachers, contribute to the community of learning that is being formed. In addition, the content that a teacher chooses to include in the critical first days of school and how it is communicated establish the foundations for the social and instructional climate of the classroom. This chapter offers several practical ways that teachers can initiate and foster a positive learning experience for students.

INCLUDE THE HUMAN ELEMENT IN YOUR TEACHING

Although teachers are passionate about subject matter, most teachers do not choose to enter the teaching profession strictly to disseminate knowledge. There is a human element to teaching that motivates teachers to dedicate their lives to this rewarding, yet challenging profession. Those who are passionate about teaching hold on to the hope that their work will make a difference in the life of a child. Thus, it is important for teachers to show the students that they care about them as much, if not more, than the subject matter and schedule. When teachers only preview the subject matter on the first day of class and ignore or forget to connect with the students on a personal level, they are leaving out the human element of teaching. William Butler Yeats stated, "Education is not the filling of a pail but the lighting of a fire." This quote reminds us as teachers to regard the students in our classrooms as highly as we do our craft. This may mean that academic learning time will involve personal introductions, student-centered activities, structured social interaction, and class discussion. Even with the current academic climate emphasizing standardized instruction, in the end, it is the personal connections that teachers make, combined with their teaching expertise, that build the foundation for high-quality teaching and effective classroom management.

This section offers some practical suggestions for how teachers can make personal connections with their students in the first days of school.

Make Connections Before School Starts, If You Can

Connecting with students before school starts by sending them postcards or calling their homes is one way that teachers can include the human element in their teaching in a practical way and establish a personal link before school even starts. This detail may be more feasible for elementary school teachers than secondary teachers because of the difference in the number of students, but making connections with students before school starts is an extra effort that makes a difference. When my son started kindergarten, his teacher sent all her students a postcard letting them know that she was looking forward to the school year. Not only was my son excited to receive a piece of personal mail, but this also contributed to increasing his enthusiasm for the first day of school. Another elementary school teacher whom I know makes personal phone calls to each of her students before the school year begins. This makes an unforgettably positive first impression of the teacher to both the students and their families. I first learned of making connections before school starts from Ron Clark, Disney's 2001 Teacher of the Year Recipient. He actually makes home visits in Harlem, in New York City, and explains his goals for the year to each family. Although Mr. Clark's efforts to connect with his students are extraordinary, any efforts to make connections with students before school starts are meaningful and appreciated.

Learn Student Names Immediately

Learning the students' names immediately is a practical way that teachers can make efforts to connect personally with the students. One way to learn the students' names on the first day of class is to incorporate some type of interactive activity that will lower students' affective levels, give them opportunities to meet their classmates, and help them to feel more comfortable in class. This is an extremely important activity on the first day of class because it helps students to feel that they belong, contribute to, and are now members of a shared community. When considering Maslow's hierarchy of needs (1968), which begins with *physiological, safety,* and *belonging* needs and ascends to *esteem* and *self-actualization,* it is clear that the basic human needs of security and belonging should be met first before an individual moves on to more complex, intellectual actions. An introductory activity does not have to be complicated; it may be as simple as having each student introduce himself or herself and share something unique, like place of birth or special talent. These personal bits of information allow all members in the community to find a common point from which to begin relationships and to build teamwork within a classroom. In providing these moments, the teacher and the students of the classroom community are socially constructing meaning in their environment and investing in a community of learning. This is a valuable investment of time in the management, discipline, and motivation of the overall classroom. A personal list of easy and fun ways for students to introduce themselves can be compiled by simply asking others from both inside and outside the world of education for suggestions, making notes from parties or workshops one has attended, or by doing a quick search on the Internet for icebreakers. The following activity is one that has been successfully used in my classrooms for student introductions and helps to initiate personal connections and conversations with and among the students.

Two Truths and a Lie

Playing "Two Truths and a Lie" is a way to help learn the students' names along with a piece of information about each of them. Students write two things that are true and one that is a lie about themselves on a 3x5 card, and then the students stand by their desks while they introduce themselves and share their two truths and their lie. The class then has to decide what the lie is, and everyone quickly engages in informal, personal, and rather comical interactions. Students are often very creative with their truths and lies and reveal facts about themselves that they consider interesting or important. It is best for teachers to model the activity by starting out with their own two truths and one lie and seeing if the students can detect the lie. Here is an example:

1. I can speak three languages fluently.

2. I do not like to touch any red sauces, like ketchup, or I will feel nauseated and sick!

3. I was once the voice of a cartoon character.

It is important to take the time to go back and review the names that have been introduced after each 4–5 introductions, so that the students are learning all the names along with the teacher, and the class is building its body of knowledge together. Repetition and review are critical steps in this activity.

After engaging in this exercise, all students will leave the first class knowing the first and last names of some, if not all, of their classmates. The students and the teacher also conclude the class with a smile and a positive first impression of the class. The groundwork for building a sense of a safe community where the students can gather to learn together has been laid.

Explore Students' Interests Through Personal Conversations

Understanding students is a standard commonly found on lists of national teaching standards. Getting to know students' cultures, interests, and upbringings helps teachers to understand whom they are teaching and how to relate to the students better. Expressing an interest in the personal side of students' lives tells the students that teachers are interested in them as people and not just as students to whom content instruction is delivered. It is interesting and amazing to uncover all the talents and cultures that lie in our students. Besides just talking about school activities, teachers should ask students about their personal interests outside of school. When students introduce themselves at the beginning of the year, it is a good idea to try and uncover some of their personal interests and then to keep those bits of information in mind throughout the year for motivational purposes. For instance, if a specific sport, talent, or place of interest is discussed, then teachers should consider incorporating it into the class reward system. In addition, if students enjoy listening to a particular type of music or playing a particular instrument, then the teacher could play some music in class that related to their interests. Taking time to uncover student interests by engaging in personal conversations with them builds community within the classroom and helps teachers reveal and cultivate the personal side of teaching.

Stay Hip, or "In the Know"!

Students also appreciate it when teachers are in tune with pop culture or the current events of their worlds. This dimension of teaching is unexplainably powerful. Recognizing popular musical groups, cartoon characters, video games, fashion trends, or reality shows, and then incorporating them into your teachings and conversations is highly appreciated and well noted by students. This also aids teachers' understandings of the culture their students are growing up in and helps teachers to note the differences found that may affect teaching and learning. The admiration or respect gained from the students because teachers have stayed hip or "in the know" contributes to the positive atmosphere created in the classroom and connects the students and teacher in a way that builds rapport with the students and fosters a sense of community. In such a positive environment, a classroom can be managed and run more smoothly and effectively.

SHARE EXPECTATIONS

At the beginning of the year, it is essential for teachers to communicate clearly with the students what is expected from them in the classroom. This may be done in the form of a written contract, a poster on the wall, or both. The important point here is that the teacher's expectations be clearly delineated. Then, throughout the year, it is the responsibility of both the teacher and the students to maintain these standards.

This section presents useful ways that expectations can be shared between teachers, students, and parents.

List Your Essentials: Be Clear About Your Expectations

At both the elementary and secondary levels, the initial days of school are the ideal times for teachers to share their expectations with the students and to set the guidelines, rules, and procedures for the classroom. Some teachers take the time to have the students contribute to the class rules and post a collaborative list in the class throughout the year. I have a personal list of essentials, or rules that are important to me in my classroom, and I share these with my students on the first day so that they know what can and cannot be done in my classroom. My list includes items like turning off cell phones while in class, not taking things off of my desk, and not chewing gum in class. I think that every teacher should stop and make a list of their essentials before meeting their first class and then communicate them clearly to the students. This orderly structure and clear communication sets the initial foundation for a successful discipline plan.

Ask Students to Articulate Their Expectations

At the onset of class, it is also important for students to share their expectations with the teacher. It is helpful for teachers to know what the students' expectations of the class are, as well as some personal information about the students. For homework on the first day of class, having the students reflect and respond to a Course Expectations Questionnaire is both interesting and insightful. A questionnaire example is provided in the next section. The questions can be modified for elementary-age students, and depending on grade level, the activity could be completed in class or at home. Upper-grade students may be more likely to work independently and be able to articulate their responses, whereas primary students may need more guidance and scaffolding. Secondary level students can respond to the questions as a homework assignment during the first week of school. Encourage the students not to simply write the responses to the questions on a sheet of college-ruled paper. Instead, tell them to make a good first impression by presenting the answers in some creative form that shows off their personality. For example, a star basketball player could write the answers on a basketball. An artistic student could make a CD cover and then have the tracks list be a brief response to each question. Teachers will be amazed at how creative the students are and the information revealed from this first day's activity will leave an impression on the whole class! When expectations are made clear for both parties, the possibilities for success increase tremendously.

Have Students Complete a Course Expectations Questionnaire

The following is a list of suggested questions to prompt students as they articulate their course expectations and describe themselves at the beginning of school:

1. Describe your expectations for this class. What do you expect to learn in this class? (Take time to consider how you might be left disappointed not learning something.) Be as specific as possible.

2. How much time do you *think* will be needed to be devoted to this class outside of the regular class meetings? How much time are you *willing* to give?

3. What kind of learner are you (visual, audio, or kinesthetic)?

4. If you were a teacher, how would you make learning fun?

5. What makes a course "challenging" for you?

6. What do you consider to be a reasonable amount of homework?

7. What do you like about yourself?

8. What don't you like about yourself?

9. List any hobbies or activities you are involved in, or any special awards you have received.

10. What is really important to you? (Or who?)

11. Share something "weird" about yourself! (For example: I don't eat anything white.)

12. Share any of your personal background or goals that you have for yourself this year.

Ask Parents to Share Their Perspectives and Expectations

Another exercise that has proven to be helpful for both elementary and secondary teachers is to request that parents or caregivers write the teacher a letter at the beginning of the year that describes their child in a personal way. The content of the letter should help teachers learn special characteristics of the students as well as their most effective learning modalities. Although this type of letter is more commonly requested from parents of elementary school students, the insights that these letters can offer about secondary students would also prove to be extremely helpful to teachers. Parents should also describe the expectations they have for their child's school year in these letters, and teachers could use the information when discussing the student's progress during conferences. These letters paint a picture of the students that offers teachers great insights into the most effective ways to teach and to get to know the students more personally.

Have Parents Write a Descriptive Letter About Their Child

The following is a sample letter that can be written to the parents to request such a letter:

Date

Dear Parents,

I am thankful for this opportunity to be your child's teacher this year. I look forward to a year filled with lots of fun and learning. Our year will pass by quickly, and in order for me to maximize the learning in our classroom during our short year together, it will be very helpful for me to learn about the personal characteristics of your child. I would appreciate it if you could write me a personal letter sharing your child's interests, friends, hobbies, strengths, and special needs. The letter does not have to be long, or typed, and it will be read by only me. Any personal insights that you can offer are very valuable to me as I share this journey of helping your child learn and grow.

Gratefully,

[Signature]

La Fecha

Estimados Padres,

Estoy agradecida para esta oportunidad a ser la maestra de su hijo/a este año. Tengo mucha anticipación para un año muy divertido y lleno de aprendizaje. Nuestro año pasará rápidamente, y para hacer lo máximo que puedo como maestra durante nuestro año corto juntos, me ayudará mucho a aprender sobre las características personales de su hijo/a. Les pido a Uds. que me escriban una carta personal describiéndome los intereses, los amigos, los pasatiempos, las fuerzas, y las necesidades especiales de su hijo/a. La carta no tiene que ser larga, ni escrita a máquina, y sólo yo voy a leerla. Cualquier perspectiva personal que pueden ofrecerme es valiosa a mí mientras yo preparo a ayudarle a su hijo/a a aprender y crecer este año.

Muchas gracias,

[Signature]

From reading these letters, teachers can better understand the student and parent perspectives and can then share with them how the class is or is not geared to fulfilling their expectations.

TAKE PRIDE IN YOUR CLASSROOM

Taking pride in one's classroom is a detail that contributes to the positive first impressions that are formed of teachers and their classes. If a teacher's work area looks unorganized or if efforts to display student work or showcase bulletin boards appear lacking, this can send the wrong message to those who enter the room. However, if a teacher pays attention to the details of creating a motivating learning environment for students, this can help build community and pride throughout the classroom. Showing pride in one's workspace by including student work, students' pictures, and motivational quotes throughout the room should not be underrated. Adding these details to a teacher's classroom promotes admiration and respect for the teacher and builds positive relationships between students and teachers. Seeing their pictures and work neatly displayed on the walls also gives students a sense of belonging to the community of learning that is being established in the classroom. We are all beings who are affected by visual stimuli, and taking pride in one's classroom sets the stage for maximized and positive learning.

TEACH LIFE LESSONS

Often, I pause in my preservice classes to teach my students "life lessons." These are lessons that have a connection to our classroom but can also be applied to life in some way. I use the activity "Sharing Expectations" in the first week of class as a prime opportunity to introduce one of my first life lessons by pointing out to the students that sharing expectations is important not only in our classroom but also in life. I explain to students how I see the value of sharing expectations in managing relationships in my life. For the older students at the secondary levels, any time you can give them advice on relationships or dating, you have their full attention! In my personal example, I shared that when I go on a trip with my husband, I ask him at the onset of our trip what he would like to do during the trip, and then I share my vision for the trip. This way, in the end, neither of us is left disappointed that we did not get the chance to do what we wanted to do. We have both had the opportunity to communicate honestly about our expectations for our time together, and we can then work together more effectively to manage our time in such a way that both our expectations can be met. Students appreciate when teachers move beyond textbook knowledge to teach life lessons; these are often the lessons that leave the most lasting impression.

BE CAREFUL NOT TO JUDGE A STUDENT'S POTENTIAL FOR LEARNING ON THE BASIS OF YOUR FIRST IMPRESSIONS

As human beings, we are visual creatures who naturally seem to judge people by their physical appearance. Although I accept that this behavior is an automatic response, I also believe that it is a human flaw of which we must be careful. Teachers' attitudes can be detrimental to students' learning if teachers judge them on the basis of first impressions of physical appearance. Because students do not fit into a prefabricated mold of an ideal student image, teachers could potentially limit their opportunities for learning. For instance, students who are English-language learners and have difficulties with language, or students from low socioeconomic backgrounds who appear unkempt, could be predestined and wrongly labeled as students of low ability due to their cultural influences. However, these very students could be the ones who flourish and become academic champions if given the opportunity, the support, and the confidence.

To model this life lesson to my preservice students, on the first day of my educational psychology class at the university, I roleplay my mother. She is a South Korean immigrant who speaks with a heavy accent and broken English. I pull my hair back and wear an interesting ensemble: a long black wool skirt, a pilgrim-collared oversized suit with shoulder pads, a bright magenta and gold-colored paisley printed scarf, tube socks over dark nylons, and sandals. I know my students are all looking at me aghast because I am a walking fashion violation. The majority of the students appear frustrated as they struggle to understand my exaggerated accent. Some students give up trying to understand my speech and respond rudely with quick, short answers and disgusted facial expressions. Others are sweetly empathetic, and these are the students who smile and nod their heads to encourage me and then speak slowly and loudly in response to my questions. I teach my students on that first day of class that people have the potential to learn and to be very intelligent even if they wear clothes that may not fit, that may not be in fashion, or even do not speak English fluently and have a thick foreign accent. What shocks my students is when I begin to peel my mother's wardrobe off in the middle of class while my own clothes are on underneath her ensemble. I then begin to speak without her broken accent, and then the lesson really hits home to them as they individually begin to realize how their perspectives of me have changed instantaneously because I have changed my wardrobe and my language. Why do I do this? Because I believe that it is important to teach others, especially future teachers, that though we are all human and are quick to judge people on the basis of our first impressions of them, we are sadly limiting our perception of their abilities before even giving them a chance. For a teacher, this preconceived expectation of a student's abilities based solely on an initial visual representation of an individual can end up actually limiting what is learned. We should remember that all human beings have the potential to learn, even though they might not meet all the expectations of the essential qualities of a person that we have already conjured up in our minds.

In my own teaching, I believe I have fallen prey to this inappropriate habit of quick judgment, and it is from learning from my mistakes that I am able to include this life lesson in this book. Although I serve as the role model as the teacher in my classroom, my students are also my teachers, and each year I learn many valuable lessons from them. I have watched students and teachers gawk, laugh, limit, and criticize students who resemble the stereotypical Hispanic gang member, or the student with attention deficit disorder who comes to school each week with different colored hair, or the student from a foreign country whose clothes are not stylish, or the neglected student who smells and whose clothes do not fit anymore but whose parents have not noticed. From this group, I have seen come forth academic champions and responsible, professional, contributing members of society. These are my silent heroes because they excelled and soared to the top in spite of those, like me, who were so quick to judge their potential by their outward appearance.

In the book *Between Teacher and Child,* Ginott (1965) summarizes the powerful role that teachers play daily in the lives of students:

I am the decisive element in the classroom.

It is my personal approach that creates the climate.

It is my daily mood that makes the weather.

As a teacher I possess tremendous power to make a child's life miserable or joyous.

I can be a tool of torture or an instrument of inspiration.

I can humiliate or humor, hurt or heal.

In all situations, it is my response that decides whether a crisis will be escalated or de-escalated, and a child humanized or de-humanized.

Indeed, the way that a teacher responds to, teaches, and judges a student from the first day of school to the last will affect the student's learning as well as his or her life.

BE YOURSELF

One of the most important and practical lessons that teachers should learn before they begin their first day of teaching is *be yourself.* Although experienced teachers, administrators, and friends can all offer different pieces of advice about what they believe to be appropriate or valuable in the first days of teaching, in the end, it is the teacher's responsibility to select and form the first few lessons and activities that will best express his or her own style, standards, and self. Teachers must do what they believe is right. One student teacher intern shared with me after her first day of teaching that she tried to combine the advice of several different well-respected people when creating her first day's lesson, but afterwards, she realized that she actually did not represent her own style and personality. New teachers, especially, may feel that they need to simply trust the wisdom of experienced teachers, but they should also be encouraged to do what feels natural and is important to them. Just because they are new teachers does not mean that their instincts and ideas are not valid. Even though it is good to solicit and accept the advice of other teachers, it is equally important not to lose yourself and your own identity as a teacher in this process. Trusting one's instinct and taking time to reflect upon what is important to you personally as a teacher is very valuable. So don't forget, above all, to be yourself.

CONCLUSION

Once I attended the 10-year reunion of one of my favorite graduating high school classes, and I reconnected with one of my former students who reinforced for me the power of first impressions. As we were becoming reacquainted, he stopped to say, "Did you know that you are my first memory of high school? You were the first person I spoke to, you were my first class, my first high school teacher. . . ." I remembered that student. I remembered his first and last name. I remembered that he had a younger brother. I remembered his perfect penmanship. I remembered that he was very intelligent and an excellent student. I do not remember that first day of class. I do not remember what I wore or what exact lesson I taught. But that student, 10 years after high school, remembered that I was his first memory of high school. He remembers the personal connection I made with him and his classmates—a connection that awarded me an invitation to his class reunion 10 years later. I know that such a special and priceless invitation did not come simply because of the lessons that I taught or the classes that I disciplined, but rather from the personal relationships that were formed through this incredible profession that we call teaching.

❧ Practical Tips ❧

- Include the human element in your teaching.
- Make connections before school starts, if you can.
- Learn student names immediately.
- Explore students' interests through personal conversations.
- Stay hip or "in the know."
- Share expectations.
- List your essentials; be clear about your expectations.
- Ask students to articulate their expectations.
- Have students complete a Course Expectations Questionnaire.
- Ask parents to share their perspectives and expectations.
- Ask parents to write a descriptive letter about their child.
- Take pride in your classroom.
- Teach life lessons.
- Be careful not to judge a student's potential for learning on the basis of your first impressions.
- Be yourself.

Chapter Two

Making Time Through the Art of Multitasking

The task of the best teacher is to balance the difficult juggling act of becoming vitally, vigorously, creatively, energetically, and inspiringly unnecessary.

—Gerald O. Grow

Multitasking is a way of life for a teacher. As a classroom teacher, conducting, managing, and overseeing several activities simultaneously in any given class period is a normal practice. At the elementary level, a prime example of multitasking is the students' *center time*, which involves rotations of different activities that occur simultaneously and require the teacher's careful attention to management and preparation. Multitasking is a skill that teachers must possess to survive in this profession. There is a tremendous amount of work involved in teaching, and trying to balance professional tasks along with a personal life is extremely difficult if one's time is not managed effectively. Having worked at the elementary, secondary, and higher levels of education, I know that there is no part-time in teaching. Part-timers really work full-time, and full-timers work more than 100%. For teachers whose lives are consumed by constant grading, preparation, and nonteaching responsibilities, the art of multitasking is essential when trying to complete professional tasks and protect time for friendships, fun, and family.

Learning how to manage time effectively is a critical skill needed to balance the demands of a professional and personal life. This chapter presents practical methods for successful multitasking. These tips will help teachers find creative ways to make time so they can

- set and accomplish realistic goals,
- study (for continuing-education or graduate school courses),
- grade papers,
- leave workshops with finished products,
- maximize instructional time in their classrooms, and
- have fun.

IDENTIFY HOW YOUR TIME IS SPENT

Responsibilities and opportunities increase with age and experience; however, the minutes of days do not. Unable to change time, teachers have to learn how to manage the finite minutes of the day to complete all their necessary tasks. The first step to effective time management involves looking at one's schedule and identifying how one's time is used throughout the day. Teachers must identify their resources first before they move forward in understanding how to use them most efficiently. Then they can become creative by learning how to multitask and maximize their time. The following pages offer a process to help teachers identify how much time they have in each day, how they spend their time, and what priorities fill their time.

BE A LIST MAKER

Be a list maker, and be proud of it! To-do lists are a tangible representation of what needs to be completed in any given day or week. These lists also help teachers when they stop to evaluate how their short-term actions are contributing to their long-term goals.

Schedule-Making Exercise

Beginning teachers are commonly overwhelmed by the demanding schedule of teaching. Keeping up with grading papers, preparing innovative lesson plans, and balancing one's personal life are a challenge, and time is usually scarce. To help teachers have a better understanding of how to manage their time, this scheduling activity was created. After filling in the times on the chart when teachers are at work or are fulfilling family responsibilities, teachers can see a visual representation of how much time is actually left in a given week to carry out other professional and personal priorities. This also helps teachers to see how multitasking may be necessary to complete all the responsibilities of a given week, and when the best times to multitask may be.

List personal goals that need to be included in your weekly schedule (Table 2.1). These include basic needs like eating, so time needs to be set aside for meals. Personal priorities should also include exercise, meditation or quiet time, service activities, and time with friends or family. Afterward, fill in the activities on the timetable (Table 2.3) on the following page.

Table 2.1   *Personal Priorities*

Personal priority	Estimated time needed each week
1.	
2.	
3.	
4.	

List professional goals that need to be included in your weekly schedule (Table 2.2). This includes time for reading, professional writing, grading, and special meetings. Afterward, fill in the activities on the timetable on the following page.

Table 2.2   *Professional Priorities*

Professional priority	Estimated time needed each week
1.	
2.	
3.	
4.	

Table 2.3 *Weekly Schedule*

	Sunday	Monday	Tuesday	Wednesday	Thursday	Friday	Saturday
6–7 a.m.							
7–8 a.m.							
8–9 a.m.							
9–10 a.m.							
10–11 a.m.							
11 a.m.–12 p.m.							
12–1 p.m.							
1–2 p.m.							
2–3 p.m.							
3–4 p.m.							
4–5 p.m.							
5–6 p.m.							
6–7 p.m.							
7–8 p.m.							
8–9 p.m.							
9–10 p.m.							
10–11 p.m.							

Writing lists brings forth the thoughts from our imagination into the visuals of our real world and helps focus our time and actions. Many insightful tips to managing time can be gained from making lists, and here are three of the most important ones:

1. Set Realistic Daily Goals

When composing a list of daily tasks, teachers should also consider their schedules for the day and estimate how much time realistically exists to accomplish the listed tasks. Often, we write down five things to do for a particular day, but if we sat down to think about how long each task would take, we might realize that these were unattainable goals. For example, I was tutoring a young high school student once, and she seemed burdened by the many tasks that she had left to accomplish after she left our appointment. I asked her to describe what she had on her agenda that evening, given that it was already quickly approaching the dinner hour. Her list included eating dinner, completing at least two hours of homework for one class, studying for a test for another class, a composition, a meeting with a friend, and editing a short movie clip. I asked her to identify which tasks needed to be completed before the next day and advised that she dedicate the remainder of her evening to the assignments that had the most immediate deadlines. The movie that needed to be edited, for example, did not need to be completed until later that week. When making a to-do list for the day, always assess how long each task will take and then prioritize the activities according to their deadlines.

2. Be Intentional About How You Spend Your Time

Lists help teachers to be intentional about how they spend their time. A teacher's daily work time can be easily taken up by a number of distractions and miscellaneous activities. If important tasks, such as eating lunch or spending time with colleagues, are left off teachers' schedules, they may be easily pushed aside and never completed. At work, teachers are so focused on teaching, administrative tasks, and students that they do not always allow time for other activities that are equally important. In my case, although I believed that taking care of myself and engaging in collegiality were priorities to me, after reviewing my weekly schedule and daily lists of tasks, I realized that I did not allocate much time in my busy days at work to these activities. It was an epiphany for me to stop and make time to eat and spend time with colleagues. Now, though it may seem odd to list eating lunch and talking to certain colleagues on my to-do list, that is how I get it done. So maybe it's not so odd after all.

3. Keep Focused

A wise colleague once advised, "If what you are engaged in does not help you with your long-term goal, then you should not waste your time on it." New teachers, in particular, may find it difficult to stay focused in their early years in teaching. This may largely be due to the fact that extra duties aside from teaching, like coaching, club advising, and committee work, are typically offered to the new teachers, and because they want to make a good impression, beginning teachers feel compelled to take on these extra activities. However, in their early years of teaching, beginning teachers should focus mainly on their teaching and on managing their classrooms well, because the primary goal should be to excel in these areas first before fragmenting oneself into other areas of the profession. In all levels of the teaching profession, there are many opportunities to give one's energy to activities outside of teaching. But the key is to stay focused on the larger goals and to be able to discern what may simply distract you from what is truly important. It is understandable for a new teacher's lists to consist mainly of items that are related to lesson preparation and classroom management, so if a beginning teacher's daily work mainly involves extracurricular tasks, an adjustment of priorities or time devoted to teaching may be needed.

Making lists is a practical way for teachers to set realistic daily goals, to be intentional about how they spend their time, and to evaluate their priorities.

FIND CREATIVE TIMES TO READ

Reading—whether it is reading for continuing-education classes, graduate school, or to prepare for one's classes—is something for which a teacher must find or make time. I can remember when

I was attending graduate school, I was faced with mountains of reading. At the time, I had a one-year-old son, was teaching Spanish classes at our local high school, and was the chair of the Department of Foreign Language. Needless to say, finding time to read and study was hard. Yet, though difficult, it was not impossible. Like any new teacher I needed a plan. By carefully analyzing one's weekly schedule and brainstorming ways to solve specific time crunches, it is possible to find solutions. Taking on a *positive, determined attitude* is critical. If you feel defeated before even trying to tackle whatever needs to be done, then you may have already closed your mind to all the creative opportunities that lie before you.

My solution: In order for me to complete my reading, I joined a gym! While I rode on the stationary bicycle, I completed my homework and teaching preparation, and my son was being well cared for in the child-care center of the gym. This was more affordable than hiring a babysitter just so that I could read, because my gym membership already included babysitting. So, I was able to stay in shape, keep up with my homework, and make sure that my son was taken care of all at the same time. Not every new teacher has a new baby, but we all bring personal commitments to our demanding work and need to get creative about reconciling competing demands.

Another tip for fitting in reading is just to have reading materials in the car or with you always to soak up time whenever it is found during the day. When teachers find themselves waiting—in a car pickup line for kids after school, in the doctor's office, or at the car wash—having something to read close by can sponge up extra time. It is amazing to see how much reading can be done during these dead times throughout the day. Listening to books on tape to catch up on leisure reading while driving or exercising is also a constructive use of time. Ordinary slots of time can be transformed in a productive way if you think ahead and are prepared.

TAKE YOUR PAPERWORK EVERYWHERE

Most teachers list grading or paperwork as one of the negative aspects of teaching. Once again, the piles of homework to read, correct, and record seem endless, and with a limited amount of time given in each day, it is difficult to find the time to get it all done. Just as efficient teachers take their reading everywhere, they take students' papers everywhere.

It is important to note that there are appropriate and inappropriate times to work on grading, and although I do not encourage grading while someone is making a presentation, it is helpful to have something to work on in case a faculty meeting has been delayed unexpectedly or the setup time is longer than anticipated. For example, once when attending a technology conference with my student teachers, we all sat in the same row of one particular session, and I looked down the aisle and saw that they had all brought their students' papers to correct and were busy grading while we waited for the speaker to set up her presentation.

LOOK AHEAD AND KILL TWO PROJECTS WITH ONE WORKSHOP

Educational workshops are settings where teachers gather to learn more about how to improve their teaching craft using some new tool or knowledge. Usually it is understood that in an educational workshop, the instructor will have the participants create a final product using the information that is taught, or will encourage the participants to use the information in their classrooms in some way. Often, workshop attendees will learn the material while in class and then hope to find the time later to create a lesson or presentation using what they learned in the workshop. However, finding the time to actually return to these endeavors is difficult and realistically not plausible. These workshops can be more productive and efficient when teachers brainstorm in advance either individually or collectively on classroom applications to use *while in the workshop* and go to the workshops prepared to readily apply the knowledge in a practical way. This may entail some prior preparation on the teacher's part to bringing the appropriate materials to the workshop to help get started.

When attending any workshop, try to create a related lesson plan or something practical to use in your classroom or even in your life *during* the workshop time. Before attending technology workshops, for example, try to think of ways to use the application you are going to learn to create and complete a project during the workshop time rather than just playing around with the software without any project in mind. Once when taking a workshop for advanced PowerPoint, I brought along digital pictures of my family on my flashdrive and used the pictures in my working project as I learned about how to use the advanced features of PowerPoint. By the end of the workshop, I had created a PowerPoint presentation for my husband for Father's Day. So, I not only learned PowerPoint, but I also made a gift. When there is so much time dedicated to keeping up with one's professional life as a teacher, many teachers often find it challenging to keep up with personal items like gift-giving for special occasions. In addition to creating a gift, by using the workshop knowledge immediately to create something that had importance for me, I internalized the skills much more effectively so that I could later incorporate them more quickly and confidently into my teaching.

It is important to be a sponge for good teaching ideas wherever you find them so that you do not need to come up constantly with creative strategies for engaging students from scratch. At a continuing-education health class I attended, the instructor used a *Hollywood Squares* game format to quiz us on the material at the end of the day. When I left that class, I had not only learned more about health issues in classrooms, but I had also jotted down titles and questions that I could use in my own classroom using the *Hollywood Squares* game format modeled that day. As teachers, we are all constantly learning, and we need to take these opportunities in continuing education to apply this knowledge in a practical way to use in our own classrooms. By trying these ideas out as quickly as possible, you can keep them from becoming just another note to yourself in another pile of paper.

DELEGATE, DELEGATE, DELEGATE!

A beginning teacher can be quickly overwhelmed by all the responsibilities and tasks involved in teaching. In addition, many have a streak of perfectionism and feel that they must personally complete all the tasks involved in teaching, which includes putting names on folders, creating bulletin boards, and photocopying papers. So, one of the basic lessons that all teachers should learn and use is *Accept the help of others!* New teachers, especially, may view this as a sign of weakness, when really it is a sign of intellect. It reminds me of a saying that, "Being smart is not knowing all the right answers; it's just knowing how to get them." So, in the world of teaching, being a good teacher may not be doing it all on your own but just knowing who can help you get it all done. There are not enough hours in the day for teachers to do it all, so we must find ways to give up our perfectionism, release control, and accept help. It may not be perfect, but it can still all be completed well. Accepting help from others is a practical way of multitasking. While you are working on one thing, if you can, give someone else another task to complete. It is okay to let go.

In certain schools, teachers can give up clerical tasks and additional classroom preparation to other people such as teachers' aides, capable students who need something constructive to do during an office aide period or study hall, or parent volunteers. Often, new teachers do not realize that these resources are available to them, and so they are left unused. The availability of such resources varies from school to school, but for some teachers, simply discovering that these treasures exist is encouraging. Even though most teachers enjoy being in control, it is an important lesson to learn early on that teachers should save as much of their energies as possible for teaching and working with the students and to delegate as much of the other work as possible to those who are able to help. When teaching elementary school, I learned that parents will often generously volunteer their time to do the cutting and pasting and book orders so that I could use that time to focus on lesson planning. Although parent volunteers are not available in all school contexts, when they are, their help should be graciously accepted. At the secondary levels, students can be recruited to be teachers' assistants (TAs) and are extremely helpful in completing clerical tasks that often take up a great deal of time after a day of teaching. Making copies, correcting multiple-choice sections of quizzes or exams, alphabetizing students' papers so it is easy to enter grades in a computer or gradebook, and making bulletin boards are just a few tasks that teachers' assistants can complete. Even students who are serving detention in the classroom can help pitch in through some of these constructive ways. It is amazing how much time all these tasks can add up to be, and although it may be difficult at first, it is a smart and critical lesson to learn to accept help when it is given, both in and out of one's classroom.

MULTITASK WHEN HANDING PAPERS BACK TO STUDENTS

Of course, multitasking is a necessary skill for managing one's classroom. Teachers must juggle a number of procedures at the same time when teaching and carrying out administrative or clerical tasks. Handing papers back to students is one task that can take up quite a bit of valuable instructional time if not handled properly. It is best to reserve this procedure for a time when students are engaged in some type of activity (e.g., a quiz, a warm-up activity, work with partners, or in-class exercises). Having students sit and be idle while teachers pass back papers is not an effective use of time. So, it is best to multitask when handing papers back to students.

PAMPER YOURSELF WITH MANY THINGS, NOT JUST ONE THING

It is important for teachers to remember to take the time to take care of themselves because if they are constantly working, burnout is inevitable. Even with fun things like pampering myself, I find myself multitasking. I may want to soak myself in a long bubble bath and also treat myself to watching a classic "chick flick" but can't find the time in a given day for both. So, I'll set up my portable DVD player or laptop computer on the counter in the bathroom and play the video while soaking in all the bubbles. I think what I am really doing here is soaking up my time with two wonderful things rather than just one. Multitasking is a beautiful thing when it comes to work or play.

CONCLUSION

I have found that teachers are the most resourceful people I have met. I see them convert the most ordinary objects into creative projects for their classrooms. For example, elementary school teachers recycle frozen-food containers into paint palettes for art lessons, and they use mismatched puzzle pieces to glue together a beautiful brooch or to make picture frames that say, "I love you to pieces!" for Mother's Day presents. In this same way, teachers should handle their time in a creative fashion. It seems like such an ordinary resource: We all have it. But it is how we use our time that makes us different. In the teaching profession, learning how to maximize the finite minutes of the day will help teachers not only survive but thrive in this challenging career. With simple steps like keeping papers or reading materials close by, ordinary waiting time can be transformed into well-managed, constructive time. Although we cannot change the amount of time in each day, we can change our perspective and accept what is given to us and use it creatively and resourcefully through the art of multitasking.

❧ Practical Tips ❧

- Identify how your time is spent.
- Set realistic daily goals.
- Be intentional about how you spend your time.
- Keep focused.
- Keep books or papers with you so that you can take advantage of creative times to read.
- Take your paperwork everywhere so that you can grade during dead times throughout the day.
- While you are in a workshop, focus on projects that you will actually use. Don't count on having the time afterward to begin the project.
- Delegate, delegate, delegate!
- Accept help.
- Multitask when handing papers back to students.
- Treat yourself to many good things.

CHAPTER THREE

Making Grading Manageable

Hard work is often the easy work you did not do at the proper time.

—Bernard Meltzer

O ne of the greatest challenges that teachers face is learning how to handle grading. Although a typical school day ends between 2 p.m. and 4 p.m., a teacher's work is usually just beginning at this time. After combining the time needed to prepare future lessons, set up for the following day, and keep up with grading, little time remains for much else. For beginning teachers especially, grading can be viewed like bacteria that continue to grow uncontrollably and become all-consuming, eating away at teachers' personal lives, unless proper measures are taken. This chapter presents practical ideas for grading that will help reduce a teacher's workload and make grading a manageable and meaningful task.

There are three main tasks for teachers that involve grading: (1) grading homework, (2) grading tests or special projects, and (3) completing progress report and report card grades. Below are suggestions for how elementary and secondary teachers can successfully manage each of these categories. Some tips may overlap between the grade levels, whereas others are distinct to the elementary or secondary classrooms.

CAUTIONS ABOUT HOMEWORK

When assigning homework, teachers should understand what the purpose of homework is. Homework should be used to reinforce concepts and skills that are taught in class. Often, teachers attempt to introduce brand-new material to students through homework assignments, and this ends up being a frustrating or nonproductive use of students' time. In addition, teachers should be mindful of the specific objectives they wish to reinforce with homework and consider whether the assignment is a reasonable means of achieving the objectives. For example, if an objective is to reinforce computational skills in math, this may be fulfilled with one sheet of math problems. The caution here is not to overload students with excess worksheets that reinforce the same objective.

It is also important for teachers to consider the time left in a given day for students to complete homework, especially if students are involved in athletic programs or other extracurricular activities. When we stop to consider the daily schedule of a secondary student involved in some type of afterschool activity, we will quickly discover that if these students go to bed before 10 p.m., they may only have three hours to complete homework for six classes every evening. This would allow the students to spend only 30 minutes on an assignment for each class. So, teachers should consider what a realistic expectation for time invested in homework is. At the elementary level, the same idea applies. For instance, if students have two working parents, homework may not be attended to until after dinner time, which leaves about two hours. In addition, teachers should take into account that not all parents or caregivers at home are able to assist students with homework. Language barriers and cultural differences of families vary the resources that students have at home. Therefore, when assigning homework, teachers should be mindful of what specific objectives are being reinforced, what a reasonable time investment is for attaining the objective, and what resources are available at home for students. It is good practice for teachers to complete the homework pages themselves so that they can be sure that all the concepts were taught and that there are no errors in the homework pages. Sometimes teachers photocopy pages from a workbook without reading through the assignment, and the concepts addressed in the homework are not aligned with what was taught in class. Carefully reviewing homework before it is sent home will ensure that the assignment is reasonable and appropriate.

GRADING HOMEWORK: ELEMENTARY

How Are Homework Packets Constructed?

Elementary school teachers typically assign homework in one of two different ways: through either a homework packet handed out at the beginning of the week, or a weekly calendar or agenda book that is filled in with daily assignments. The first option usually involves a homework folder that is filled with a packet of assignments that is sent home on Monday and due at the end of the week. A helpful tip is to mount a brightly colored HOMEWORK FOLDER cover to a large manila envelope so that it can be easily located, and then to laminate the folder so that it is durable enough to last throughout the semester. It is also a good idea to put the due date for the homework on the cover sheet to help parents remember when it is due (i.e., homework folder due back EVERY FRIDAY). Usually after one semester, new homework folders need to be made for young students. For students who are heavily involved in sports, the homework packet is an attractive option because the homework can be completed in one evening or scheduled around days when extracurricular activities consume the afternoons and evenings.

For upper-grade students, weekly homework calendars or agenda books are used. Because these students are older and are beginning to practice more independence, daily assignments can be given and recorded on a weekly calendar or agenda book and then signed by a parent.

How Much Homework Should Be Assigned?

For students of elementary levels, homework exercises give students opportunities to practice responsibility. Students at the primary level may have about 10–15 minutes of homework per day, along with 10–15 minutes of daily reading, whereas homework in the upper grades becomes more complex or cognitively challenging and will take longer. The amount of homework assigned may vary depending on the state or school district, so it is best to check these respective guidelines.

How Is Homework Graded?

Because homework at the elementary level is intended to be used as an exercise in practicing responsibility, a qualitative approach to grading is called for at this level. Using a class roster, mark an X next to a student's name to note completion of the homework, whereas a / (slash) denotes incomplete work. A parent volunteer can process, grade, and record homework packets for the teacher. Immediate feedback to the parents and students is important when processing homework.

GRADING HOMEWORK: SECONDARY

How Are Homework Assignments Graded?

One of the fundamental questions that beginning teachers need answered is, How should homework be graded? Although there is no universal, standardized grading procedure that is implemented by all teachers, the five-point scale that I have implemented in my own secondary classrooms is easy to use and understand.

Homework was assigned daily in my high school Spanish classroom. A typical assignment consisted of approximately one to two pages of simple exercises. If the assignment exceeded this amount, then the points were easily doubled. In the classroom, a poster hung on the wall that defined each numerical value of the homework grading system:

5: Excellent. Exercises all completed on time. Corrections carefully made.

4: Very Good. Exercises were almost complete; may be missing one or two items. Minor corrections overlooked.

3: Good. Half of assignment was completed. Average number of corrections were completed.

2: Poor.   Less than half of assignment was completed. Several corrections overlooked.

1: Very poor.   Only a few attempts to begin the assignment. Majority of corrections were not completed.

Grading the students' homework began at the onset of the class period. As students settled down in their seats to complete the warm-up activity, I walked around the classroom stamping each student's homework to indicate that the assignment was completed. To receive the full credit (5 points) for the assignment, students needed a stamp. If sections of the assignment were missing, I noted the missing pieces on the student's work by writing the numbers that were missing or marking a slash on the exercises that were not completed. Because checking the homework occurred at the beginning of the period, students were unable to finish any incomplete work before I arrived at their desk. After this process, I reviewed the homework with the students briefly, allowing them to make revisions before the assignment was turned in for credit. Afterward, the assignment was handed in for me to review and to assign a quick grade of 1–5, or 1–10 if the assignment was longer. With much practice, I could soon easily spot a "5" paper or a "2" paper.

Keep in Mind Students' Special Needs and Schedules When Determining a Due Date for Homework Assignments

When teachers determine a due date for homework assignments, it is important that they consider the abilities of students with special needs or atypical school schedules. Though it may seem feasible from the teacher's perspective for students to have a task completed for the next school day, some students may need a longer time period to accomplish the work. For instance, during one day of the first week of my Spanish 1 high school class, the Spanish alphabet was introduced, and that evening's assignment was to memorize the alphabet in its entirety so that it could be recited orally in class the next day for a quiz grade. When I gave this assignment I did not consider the difficulties of students with special needs and the challenges they faced with memory skills or auditory processing. It would have benefited them to have the weekend to review and practice the alphabet, but I just mistakenly assumed that all students could accomplish this task in the same time frame that I could. Teachers should be cautioned not to assume that their students possess the same learning modalities and skills that they do. This, in addition to the special schedules of divorced families, working families, and student athletes, should be noted when determining the due dates of homework assignments. Many times, the case may be that the students can complete the work assigned, but it is just not realistically possible given the time frame that the teacher has given. After I learned from the lesson above, students were given the weekend to practice their alphabet, and others were able to recite it sooner on a voluntary basis, if they mastered it before the weekend. Giving the students this extra time helped to decrease the tension that the students with special needs or unusual schedules had felt, and the chances for student success were maximized. If these special factors are considered, successful outcomes for learning are more likely to be achieved by all students.

HANDLING EXTRA CREDIT

Teachers should be careful when dealing with extra-credit assignments. This can be an extremely controversial topic in schools, especially given the current standards-based climate of education. For instance, if a student fails to complete homework that addresses a state standard and then completes extra-credit assignments that do not address the same objectives, then certain standards for the course have not been met. Students might opt for extra-credit assignments in lieu of completing their required assignments. Teachers do not want to send this mixed message to the students or have students' grades not reflect a true assessment of their achievement. So, extra-credit assignments should not be presented as assignments that students can complete to replace their regular work. Teachers should be clear about when and how extra credit is offered, or aggressive parents and students might take advantage of the situation. My suggestion is not to offer extra credit regularly, or students will be classically conditioned to expect it. I have used extra credit as a motivational tool for students to answer a "bonus" question on a test, or as a means for students to learn a little more than what is required by a standard so that they are rewarded for that extra effort. In general, it is good practice not to use extra credit so much that it is the determining factor between two letter grades.

TIME-SAVING TIPS

The following time-saving grading tips can help teachers of both elementary and secondary levels to manage grading homework.

Spot-Check the Homework as It Is Being Graded

As we corrected the homework in class, I would often walk around and make personal contact with students, and spot-check their papers. This helps to save time in the long run on grading by doing some in class while I am reviewing the answers along with my students. I can observe and also mentally take note of which problems or topics were the most difficult for the students, and I make sure to check those carefully after they are handed in to be graded.

Review Only the Essential Questions

Due to time constraints, it is often difficult to review every question from the homework assignment. So, to maximize the use of the homework review time, the teacher should select the questions that appear to be the most challenging, or students should be asked which items they would like to review.

Lottery: Collect and Grade Only a Certain Number of Items

To vary grading practices, a novel technique is to have students complete a number of exercises, and then to select a couple of students to call out numbers that correspond to a few questions that will be graded for credit. This practice would be helpful for math teachers especially when assigning multiple problems for homework, or social science and language arts teachers who have assigned a number of comprehension or reflection questions from readings.

Give Quizzes in Which They Can Use Their Homework and Count the Quiz for Homework Points

To check for understanding of content but also to hold students accountable for completing their homework, allow students to use their homework assignment during a quiz and then assign the quiz homework points.

Partner Students Up for Classroom Assignments

By having students partner with another classmate to complete an assignment, teachers can reduce their grading load by half the regular quantity. In addition, students benefit from socially constructing their learning through the collaborative process of working with a partner.

GRADING TESTS OR SPECIAL PROJECTS: ELEMENTARY AND SECONDARY

Make Projects and Tests Meaningful

At both the elementary and secondary levels, educators should keep the big picture in mind when assessing students and assigning special projects. What do you really want students to remember for the long term, not just for short-term purposes of completing an assignment? For example, typical cultural projects for foreign language classes may involve having students orally present encyclopedia information about a country, such as the highest mountain range, the population size, or ethnic makeup of the land. Yet the probability of students retaining such factual information is low. By giving the students some choices and room for creativity, teachers maximize learning.

In my own Spanish class, when assigning the culture presentation, I gave students the opportunity to choose their own Spanish-speaking country. Afterward, the students had to explain why they chose that particular country, and then they chose one particular theme about the country, constructed a well-organized presentation about the theme, and presented a creative demonstration. So, a young man who was extremely interested in soccer selected Peru as his country, created a video montage of soccer in South America, and brought in a soccer ball that had been made out of white T-shirts to demonstrate how impoverished children in Peru play soccer without proper equipment. Almost 10 years later, I still remember the young man's presentation. The objective of learning about another Spanish-speaking culture was met, and in an unforgettable way.

Use Rubrics

In my own experience and observations, I have found that teachers have certain expectations or standards for student work, but these ideas are often not translated clearly to the students. As a result, when the student work is handed in, points are lost because the students did not comply with the teacher's expectations. In addition, when the grade is given, teachers may not indicate from what areas the points were deducted. So, for a project that is worth 100 points, a student may have earned a total score of 87, but where the 13 points were deducted from is unclear. Rubrics are a perfect solution to ambiguous grading. At both the elementary and secondary levels, when projects or presentations are created, take time to consider what categories will be evaluated; for example, in my work with Spanish classes, the oral presentations were typically broken up into categories like grammar, content, pronunciation, and preparedness and organization. The points, depending on the weight of the project, could then be distributed accordingly for each category. A comment column helps so that teachers can add notes about why a certain grade was given. Even with research papers, I have listed rows that clearly explain my expectations for font type, size, length of paper, and cover page. Templates and examples of rubrics are easily accessible to teachers on the Internet. When a teacher hands rubrics back to students with their project or presentation grade, it is clear to both the teacher and the student where the strengths and shortcomings of the work were found.

Grade Projects and Presentations While Students Are Giving Them in Class

Another helpful use of rubrics for grading is to mark the rubrics while students are giving their presentations in class. When

I first started out in teaching, I made notes in class but didn't mark the rubrics until later, taking away from my personal time. However, I quickly learned that I could just grade the projects and mark up or make notes on their rubrics during class, and then I would not have to take anything home with me.

GRADING TESTS OR SPECIAL PROJECTS: ELEMENTARY

Use Summative Tests

At the primary level, school districts typically use summative tests that have been developed by curriculum distributors for language arts and mathematics. Rubrics are provided with each summative assessment to help teachers score the exams. Report card grades are then determined by the summative test scoring chart. Although other items like authentic assessment and completion of homework are considered on report cards, the grades that are earned from the summative assessments are heavily weighed in the student's grade. These grade-level assessments also help the student's current teacher see how he or she measures up to particular content standards.

Test for the Long Term, and Be Mindful of Short-Term Success

In regard to math assessment, one helpful tip is not to give students a math test immediately after finishing a math unit. Often, if students complete a math chapter one day and then take the chapter test the next day, the scores are skewed because they have memorized the material and successfully retained the information in their short-term memory. However, it is recommended that teachers assess students some time later to test their retention and retrieval of the information after a longer period of time. Because teachers are challenged with time, this does not imply that months should go by; otherwise assessments would never be completed. This is simply a caution to new teachers about the fact that short-term memory recall may be higher among young people and that this should be accounted for in the testing process.

Be Sensitive to English-Language Learners When Assigning Special Projects

It can be easy to assume that all students have the resources necessary to complete special projects. Yet English-language learners, in particular, face great challenges when working on special projects not only because of their limited knowledge of the language but also because of their limited access to resources. Given these disadvantages, teachers should scaffold assignments in the following ways to help all students feel that they have equal opportunities to access the resources necessary to complete special projects:

1. *Provide an example:* Having a model or visual representation of the assignment helps all students to see what their ultimate goal is. Models are especially useful for English-language learners and provide an essential scaffold for these students in the teaching and learning process.

2. *Provide a rubric:* By listing the requirements of the assignment in a rubric, it is clear to the students what objectives need to be met to attain the optimal grade on the project.

3. *Provide class time:* Take time in class to complete certain elements of the project so that you can monitor the students' progress, as well as to give students an opportunity to borrow materials and receive the additional assistance that they may not get at home. Frequent checks of student work are also highly recommended to make sure that all students are progressing toward the end product. Taking time in class to allow students to work on their projects ensures that all students will have some element of the project completed.

4. *Provide modifications:* Using modified book report forms for English-language learners or adjusting assignments to empower the students with special needs are helpful tips for assigning special projects. If a student's strength lies in verbal expression and not in written conventions of language, the special project may need to involve an oral presentation rather than a written work. Considering these modifications promotes positive self-esteem and success in students during this crucial time in language development.

GRADING TESTS OR SPECIAL PROJECTS: SECONDARY

Don't Rely Just on the Book Tests; Read Them Ahead of Time and Adapt Them to Your Teaching Style

When beginning teachers receive their first curriculum sets, it is tempting simply to use the tests and quizzes that come along with these sets. Some prefabricated tests or quizzes may be reliable, valid instruments that assess all that you want to measure in terms of learning student outcomes; however, it is still important for teachers to preview the materials, and then also to find areas where other questions might be formulated. These might have come from a teachable moment in the classroom or from a particular teacher's unique teaching style. The point here is, Do not rely just on the book tests.

Use One Master Test With a Number System

Have one master set of exams or quizzes, and number each one to make sure that you have retrieved all copies before students leave the classroom. Many teachers are restricted to making a limited number of photocopies in a given academic year, so to be mindful of this limitation, having one master copy for an exam and asking students to use their own paper for an answer sheet is a good solution. But be sure to check each exam before giving it to the next period, just in case students wrote on them, and have backups just in case they do so you don't have to worry about erasing the markups before the next class comes in.

Make Answer Sheets to Tests That Match the Key

When grading multiple-choice or some short-answer quizzes or tests, it is helpful to make an answer sheet that matches the Master Key. This facilitates the correction process. So, if the key has 2 columns of 25 questions each, then the students' answer sheets should be structured the same way. By aligning the two documents side by side, grading can be done more quickly.

Make Two Test Forms

If teachers are concerned about cheating, especially on final exams, two versions of the exam should be made. With most exams being created using computers, a simple cut-and-paste process will quickly create two versions of the same test. Then, each pile should be numbered, and one version of the exam could be the odd group, while the other represents the even group. In these cases, it is critical to remind students to write their test number on their answer sheets, so it is clear which version of the exam they have taken. Another practical tip is to use two different kinds of colored paper when copying an exam, and then the students will be led to believe that the tests are different.

Do Not Release the Tests to the Students, and Tell Your Colleagues the Same

It is extremely time consuming to create exams. Although teachers may not use exactly the same exam the following year, it is a good practice not to let exams leave the classroom for security issues and in case a question may be repeated in the future. After students receive their grade on exams, the tests can be filed in a portfolio that is stored in the classroom for each student.

Have the High Class Average From the Weekly Test or Quiz Win a Free Homework Night

During my first year of teaching high school Spanish, I taught five Spanish 1 classes, and at the end of each week the students took a vocabulary quiz. After grading the quiz over the weekend, I wrote each class's quiz average on the board on Monday, and I rewarded the highest average by excusing them from the Monday night homework. One assignment did not make a difference in the student's overall grade, and this released me from one extra class of homework to grade. The reward motivated the students to prepare for the weekly quiz and rewarded me with a little extra time.

Stagger Projects

If you are teaching the same prep several times, stagger the due dates of large projects; this way, you may have two class sets to grade over a period of time and then two to three other class sets at a later time. Fewer students will be asking for their project grades at the same time.

Split the Final, If Possible

For Spanish classes, have students complete the oral and written portions of their exam earlier, and then, because it is the easiest portion to grade, give the multiple-choice section at the end. For English classes, have students write out their essays before the formal final exam times, and then on the day of finals, give the multiple-choice or short-answer section. This helps greatly with time management at a critical time in the semester. The trick is to not make the longest part of the exam due on the final exam day.

Pair and Share With Grading

During finals, find a colleague with whom you can partner in grading. If you each have a different prep period, he or she can run your Scantrons or grade your multiple-choice exams, and then you can return the favor. This makes grading go faster.

PROGRESS REPORTS AND REPORT CARDS: ELEMENTARY

Plan Ahead for Assessments

Elementary school teachers face a great challenge in having to assess their students on a regular basis while still managing the daily rules, procedures, and plans of a given school day. Depending on the size of a class, teachers may take up to two weeks to complete individual assessments of their students, and given that progress reports go out every four to five weeks and report cards go out three times a year, elementary school teachers must plan ahead to complete their assessments before the end of each grading period. This may entail completing assessments during lunch or during "center" time when another adult is helping with the classroom activities. It is highly recommended that teachers do not pull students out of special learning times, like art, computers, music, or physical education.

Record at Least One Grade Per Week in Each Subject

One helpful tip for elementary school teachers is to collect one item to assess for each subject matter every week. Because elementary school teachers have so many subject areas to assess, it is a challenge to gather data for assessment for each area on a regular basis. So, if teachers looked over their plan books and double-checked that weekly lessons would yield at least one piece of evidence for each subject area, this would ensure that all subject areas were covered.

How Are Grades Determined for the Report Cards?

Teachers must consider a number of factors when determining grades. Elementary school teachers review formal assessments, authentic assessments, homework, and special projects. Teachers can weight grades, in the sense that the formal assessments may have a greater impact on the student's overall grade than the homework that was completed for that subject area. The key is to communicate the grading procedures clearly to the parents and the students.

When Do Elementary School Teachers Complete Their Report Cards?

Sadly, but truthfully, progress reports and report cards are written at home or during a teacher's personal time. Unless teachers work on report cards during their lunch break, it is difficult to complete tasks like these in a given work day. Some teachers have found success in writing four to five each night to break down the task over the week.

"Cookie" Your Comments, and Build a Pool of Favorites

One of the most difficult tasks for a beginning teacher to complete in the initial years of teaching is writing comments on progress reports and report cards. Although teachers might find a student particularly challenging or needing improvement in a certain area, there is a tactful way to word these assessments without putting parents on the defensive. One helpful way to articulate the comments is to "cookie" them. With this technique, a positive comment is introduced first, followed by the constructive criticism, and then another positive comment closes the teacher's thoughts. For example, "I really enjoy having X in class. X is having difficulty matching his letters with their sounds, but he or she is extremely proficient with number recognition and will make great strides in all areas this year." After completing a number of report cards, a pool of favorite or reliable comments will begin to surface. Asking other teachers for examples of commonly used phrases in students' report cards is also an excellent way to begin mastering this practice.

Identify Remedial Students in October

To be eligible for special services during the year and to communicate with the parents at an early stage about their child's development, it is highly recommended that teachers identify students who need remediation in October. This will entail proper documentation of standardized assessments, authentic assessments, and other possible evaluations like Student Study Team. When referring students to the Student Study Team, a team of professionals that includes the student's teacher, other faculty members, special education teachers, school counselors, and administrators assess the student's abilities and recommend a plan of action so that the student can undergo the appropriate evaluations and will receive the necessary resources to maximize learning.

How Do You Assess Behavior Grades?

Students earn satisfactory grades (S), unless they have demonstrated exceptional (E) behavior that is noteworthy. Documentation of inappropriate behavior is needed if students need to improve (N) their behavior.

Explain Grades During Formal Parent Conferences

Use parent conferences to explain how grades are calculated and explain how often an evaluation of student progress will be made. Also, if parents have questions regarding their child's grade, always request that they make an appointment rather than trying to have them meet with you to discuss grades without any warning or preparation on your part. It is also advised that new teachers invite an administrator or other teacher to be present at conferences where assistance may be needed or when tensions are high.

PROGRESS REPORTS AND REPORT CARDS: SECONDARY

Have Students Guess Their Grade for Extra Credit

One of my colleagues asks her students to guess their grade in the class for extra credit. Students earn five extra credit points for guessing their grades correctly. These extra points really do not make a major difference in a student's grade; however, it motivates the students to think seriously and take time to assess their achievement in class. Students can self-assess their homework, tests, quizzes, class participation, and other special aspects of the class, such as science labs. This exercise requires the students to evaluate, reflect upon, and defend their grade in written form, and this reflection helps the students to see if their grades are valid or not. In one instance, a teacher reported that a student guessed that she earned a C+ even though she was hoping for a B–. The student's grade was a C+, and from this exercise, the grade was validated by both the student and the teacher.

Be Explicit About How the Participation Grade Is Calculated

Students can be frustrated by receiving their participation grade and not know why points were deducted. If teachers are going to include "participation" as part of the student's overall grade, then how a student will gain or lose points for participation should be made explicit. For example, if a student earns 79 points out of 100, the student should know when and why 21 points were deducted from the grade. An easy and manageable way to document student participation grades is to assign 4 points to each day of the week. In the end, each week equals 20 points, and over the course of five weeks the total number of participation points is 100 points. Typically, each quarter grading period is a five-week grading period, so assigning 4 points per day is an easy way to manage the participation points. If a student is tardy, one point can be taken away. If a student is not prepared with materials, another point can be taken away; and for differing levels of inappropriate behavior, 4–10 points can be deducted. What is important is that the earning or deduction of points be documented and communicated clearly to the student. With this in place, both the teacher and the students will be on the same page about participation points.

GRADING TIPS FOR ALL LEVELS

Back It Up

Always have a hard copy and back up your professional data on numerous devices other than your computer's hard drive. Even though computer grading programs are more of the norm in schools, it is important to have a backup or hard copy of your grades as well as your other professional material. The possibility of losing all of one's professional documents is devastating, and also very real. When teaching high school, I had kept my grades in a gradebook and then transferred them over to a grading program to be calculated. After having entered all my data before grades were due for report cards, my son, who had just began to crawl, found the power strip and pushed the power button, which turned off my computer. I had lost all the grades that I had just entered! Luckily, I had a hard copy of the grades, and this simply meant that I had to reenter them. However, imagine being a teacher who lost all the students' grades before a report card because a computer's hard drive or school's network crashed. If the data were unrecoverable, the teacher would be left without any scores to calculate grades for the students' report cards. Backing up grades is an extremely practical and important tip for all teachers.

Chunk Categories

If you are writing out your grades and you weight them by category (e.g., homework, tests, participation), write them out in chunks rather than all in a row so that you are sorting as you go along. For example, instead of simply writing all the test grades, homework assignments, and participation grades in one section, like the following:

Student	HW #1	Quiz #1	HW #2	HW #3	Quiz #2	Test #1	HW #4	HW Subtotal	Test/Quiz Subtotal
John Doe	5	18	4	4	19	89	5	18	126

Split them up into separate sections as shown below:

Student	HW #1	HW #2	HW #3	HW #4	HW Subtotal	Quiz #1	Quiz #2	Test #1	Test/Quiz Subtotal
John Doe	5	4	4	5	18	18	19	89	126

E-Mail or Phone Parents and Communicate
Early on When Students Have a Low Grade

Although progress reports are completed every five weeks, parents like to know when their children have not turned in an assignment or when their grades begin to drop. It is helpful to communicate these events to parents as soon as they occur. Also, having parents sign grade slips is a helpful practice, because progress reports often do not make it to the parents, or they come too late to remedy the problem. This helps account for those families who may not have computer access to grades and also gives teachers a form that documents that parents received the grade.

Close Grades the Week Before
They Are Actually Due

If teachers accept assignments right up to the last day of the grading period, some students' grades will not be complete if absences or makeup work is still left outstanding. So, to help alleviate this timing issue, it is helpful to calculate grades for four weeks of assignments and tests, rather than the full five weeks. This gives teachers and students a one-week makeup period to complete grades that need to be calculated for the progress report.

Don't Save the Biggest Task for
Last, or for Vacations

Do not have big projects due the last week of the semester or before vacations. Teachers will hit burnout at this stage in teaching, and having to grade large projects at these times in the semester is not helpful. In addition, families are thankful when large projects are not due after holidays. Teachers will appreciate this as well because it is easier to return to a classroom full of students who have been well rested and energized by a break, rather than already burned out and angry that they had to spend their break laboring over a project.

CONCLUSION

Grading can be an all-consuming task for teachers. Knowing the helpful tips that are described in this chapter can help alleviate some of the burdens and give teachers insights into how to manage this great responsibility successfully. Although reading and trying to adopt every helpful hint can also become overwhelming, highlighting a few bullets and adopting those practices each year is a practical and feasible way to get started. For me, just learning that I should close my high school grades the week before the grades were actually due alleviated a lot of extra stress for me as a beginning teacher. These practical tips were never presented to me in my college textbooks but have helped me tremendously to manage my grades and my sanity as a teacher.

❧ Practical Tips ❦

- Identify specific objectives of a homework assignment.
- Calculate how long it will take students to complete a homework assignment.
- Consider that not all students may have access to the same resources at home.
- Complete the homework assignment before giving it to the students.
- Use homework folders, calendars, or agenda books to manage homework in some organized fashion.
- Give students and parents immediate feedback on homework.
- Keep in mind students' special needs and schedules when determining a due date for homework assignments.
- Use extra credit sparingly and effectively.
- Spot-check the homework as it is being graded.
- Review only the essential questions when grading homework with students in class.
- Play the lottery: Collect and grade only a certain number of homework items.
- Give "quizzes" in which students can use their homework and count the quiz for homework points.
- Partner students up for classroom assignments.
- Make projects and tests meaningful.
- Use rubrics.
- Grade projects and presentations while students are giving them in class.
- Use summative tests.
- Test for the long term, and be mindful of short-term success.
- Be sensitive to English-language learners when assigning special projects.
- Don't rely just on the book tests; read them ahead of time and adapt them to your teaching style.
- Use one Master Test with a number system.
- Make answer sheets to tests that match the key.
- Make two test forms.
- Do not release tests to the students, and tell your colleagues the same.
- Have the high class average from the weekly test or quiz win a free homework night.
- Stagger projects.

- Split the final, if possible.
- Pair and share with grading.
- Plan ahead for assessments.
- Record at least one grade per week in each subject matter.
- "Cookie" your comments on report cards, and build a pool of favorites.
- Identify remedial students in October.
- Explain grades during formal parent conferences.
- Be explicit about how the participation grade is calculated.
- Back your grades up.
- Chunk grading categories.
- E-mail or phone parents and communicate early on when students have a low grade.
- Close grades the week before they are actually due.
- Don't save the biggest task for last or for vacations.

PART II

Classroom Management

CHAPTER FOUR

Reinforcing Routines and Completing Clerical Tasks

Start by doing what's necessary; then do what's possible; and suddenly you are doing the impossible.

—St. Francis of Assisi

B esides teaching one's subject matter and grade-level content effectively, managing all the procedures that are involved in running a classroom smoothly is critical to success in teaching. Although classroom management is often considered to be synonymous with classroom discipline, for the purposes of this book chapter, classroom management encompasses all the procedural and clerical tasks that teachers must handle when assuming their own classrooms. Classroom discipline can be an outcome of how a teacher manages a classroom; these disciplinary strategies are covered in the following chapter.

PROCEDURAL TASKS: MANAGING DAILY CLASSROOM ACTIVITIES

Given that there are multiple procedural tasks that teachers need to complete daily to manage lesson preparation, instruction, and homework, strategies must be implemented for teaching students to share in the responsibility of regulating these classroom procedures. This in turn, will maximize instructional time as well as a teacher's time outside the classroom. When teachers manage their classrooms well, the combination of classroom procedures and content instruction are interwoven so seamlessly that others cannot see where one begins and the other ends. This section offers helpful tips to achieve this seamless web of classroom management.

List the Agenda and Homework on the Board

Students appreciate order and clarity, and a way to establish these elements in one's classroom is to list the agenda for the day and the homework assigned for the evening on the board. Having the agenda written on the board clearly communicates how the instructional time will be spent and helps students' minds to focus on the purpose of their lessons and generates a sense of safety from knowing what to expect. Writing the homework assignments on the board also helps to minimize any disputes that might arise from unclear expectations of when an assignment is due, and it places the responsibility of knowing this information back on the students.

Create an Absent Folder for Students to Refer to on Their Own

Teachers are so consumed during classes with teaching and managing the procedures for that day that it is difficult to take time away from the daily happenings to teach students what took place when they were absent. Teachers should teach students how to self-regulate makeup work procedures when they are absent. Creating an Absent Folder that documents what was covered on specific days and stores the assignments that are distributed each day is extremely helpful. Students can go straight to the folder and see what was missed without having to approach the teacher; the agenda and extra worksheets are provided in the folder.

I still remember when I taught high school for the first time. I was so overwhelmed with teaching new lessons every day that I did not stop to think about how to document the work that I was covering for those who were absent. A student approached me one day and asked, "What did I miss last Wednesday?" and I could not remember what I had taught then. Creating an Absent Folder is the answer to this problem for the new teacher.

At the secondary level, one way to complete the Absent Folder is to ask a student each day to submit the entry for the Absent Folder. The student gathers extra worksheets, writes the day's agenda, and describes the work that was covered in class for those who will be referencing the folder for makeup work. This leaves the Absent Folder in the hands of the students. The teacher can quickly check the contents at the end of the day, but the students are responsible for maintaining the folder. Special rewards can be given to the student who contributes to the Absent Folder.

Another method is to write the names of the students who are absent on the handouts that are being passed out and then to put them in an Absent File. This way, the teacher knows that papers have been set aside for specific students who were absent. This may be done at both the elementary and secondary levels. Elementary teachers can then file the makeup exercises in the students' cubbies or homework folders.

Do Not Accept Work That Is Late or E-mailed, but Be Sensitive to Individual Cases

Depending on the grade level and the subject matter, accepting late work from students varies among teachers. In my experience, it has been a successful practice to adopt and announce the policy that late work is not acceptable and then to treat special student cases on an individual basis. When teachers announce to the whole class that late work is accepted, they create more work for themselves. This opens the door to many challenges with grading and delays the quick processing of homework assignments. Students also tend to ask teachers if homework can be e-mailed if the assignment has not been completed on time. However, when teachers agree to this procedure, they are giving up their own time to complete a task that is truly the student's responsibility. In addition, if this convenience is made publicly known to all the students of one teacher, then teachers at the secondary level could be left printing out more than 100 homework assignments on their own time. Teachers should be sensitive to the special circumstances that might arise in students' lives that may impede them from completing homework, but leaving the door wide open for late or e-mailed assignments creates more work for the teacher and releases students of their responsibilities.

Have a Weekly Work Folder

At the elementary levels, it is extremely helpful for each student to have a Weekly Work Folder. These folders are used to collect all the work completed in class that week or to return corrected homework from the prior week. This is an organized way that students' work can be gathered and returned home successfully. A volunteer parent can prepare the Weekly Work Folders to be sent home on Friday morning. The weekly work is then prepared for the students by a volunteer, and class time is not used at the end of each day for the young students to gather their work.

Have an Emergency Folder Prepared
for a Substitute Teacher

One of the difficulties that teachers face is being prepared for a substitute teacher if it becomes necessary to call in sick or not be at work for other reasons. However, life does not always give teachers the luxury of time to plan ahead for emergencies or other special circumstances that prompt teachers to miss work. So, it is highly recommended that teachers leave an Emergency Substitute Folder with the front office filled with activities and lesson plans for any given day on which the teacher may be absent (see Resources for an example substitute letter). Successful teachers always have a backup plan, or a Plan B, and the Emergency Substitute Folder is an excellent example of such a practice. The management of the classroom is clearly laid out for another teacher in case the regular teacher is faced with an emergency. Planning ahead like this is a critical component of successful classroom management.

CLERICAL TASKS: MANAGING STUDENT RECORDS AND COMPLETING PAPERWORK FOR OTHERS

Paperwork (or clerical work) can consume a teacher's job. The percentage of administrative work in teaching is excessive. These are responsibilities that student teachers can never fully assume during their teacher preparation programs, so in the early years of full-time teaching, new teachers are shocked when they realize just how many papers come across their desks or the endless number of encounters that will connect them to the office staff. Attendance, lunch count, detention, referrals, counselor summons, documentation for nurse visits, Individual Education Plans, library notices, reminders of lunch seminars, club meetings, athletic team announcements, voting for Student Council or other extracurricular functions—the list of paperwork involved in a teacher's job that has little to nothing to do with teaching subject matter knowledge is truly remarkable. Classroom routines should be established and regulated so that class time is used efficiently and managerial procedures can be carried out without taking away from instructional time or the teacher's personal time.

Ask Parents When the Best Time They Can Be Reached Is

In this highly technological age, some teachers prefer to e-mail parents, but in some instances, it is still more effective and even necessary to make phone calls. Documenting the phone calls in some organized fashion (i.e., a phone log or on an index card placed in the student's file) is highly recommended. Teachers usually gather the parent contact information at the beginning of the year. Typically, an introductory letter or classroom contract is sent home, reviewed, and signed by the parents along with sections asking for their contact information. Although it is helpful to have the parents' phone numbers, it is even more useful to have them note the best time that they can be reached. This will save teachers a great deal of time. Rather than making multiple phone calls to connect with a parent, I have been consistently successful in contacting them during the day and time that they have indicated on their information sheets. So, adding another line on the parent contact form that asks for the best time to be reached will prove to be very helpful when making parent phone calls.

Back Up Your Attendance

Although most schools use computerized attendance programs now, it is extremely helpful and highly recommended that teachers back up their attendance records in some type of daily log or folder. Computers are not completely reliable, and it is smart to have a back-up copy of your records. This also helps when teachers are talking to parents on the phone or during a parent conference. Rather than spending time to make sure that a computer is close by to view the attendance records, the teacher can quickly refer to the back-up log of attendance and see the absences and tardies that the student has accumulated. Having an attendance log is also useful when conferences are held in a place where a computer is not available (e.g., a conference room).

Complete the Lunch Count With Popsicle Sticks or Clothespins

At the elementary levels, taking lunch count is a task that can unnecessarily take up valuable class time. Teaching students how to do this task on their own can contribute to the seamless way that clerical procedures can be completed without interrupting academic instruction. Students' names can be placed on Popsicle sticks and then students can pull their stick and place it in the appropriate coffee tin that is marked "Bringing" or "Buying." Another technique is to have the students' names on clothespins and then to have them transfer their pin to the respectively labeled ribbon. With a quick glance at the sticks or pins, the teacher can note the lunch count rather than calling out each student's name and using more class time.

Just Do It

As teachers, we can very easily get so caught up and over-whelmed by the responsibilities within our classrooms, that we can neglect the background work involved in running our schools successfully. Much of this background work involves the work of the office. Many times, office staff cannot complete their jobs until they receive the teachers' responses. The attendance manager cannot complete the attendance reports until teachers send in their attendance, the counselors cannot resolve their student cases until the students are sent to the office, the Student Study Team cannot schedule the meetings until teachers complete the appropriate forms, and school report cards cannot be sent until all teachers submit their grades—the list goes on and on. To relate it to our technologically advanced world is like sending someone an e-mail message and not being able to move until a response is received. I have learned that if teachers show the staff members their respect and admiration by responding promptly and showing that they are appreciated in various ways, then they, in turn, will take care of the teachers. I believe that a teacher's reputation is built not only on their effective teaching practices in the classroom but also on their interpersonal skills in the workplace.

Therefore, here are some practical things teachers can do to help them *just do it*.

Keep a Pen in Your Box

Teachers' mailboxes hold many papers that can be instantly dealt with and returned to the appropriate staff members by simply signing the paperwork on the spot. A helpful tip is for teachers to keep a pen in their mailboxes so that they can just do it and not have to carry the paperwork back to their classrooms.

Complete Attendance at the Beginning of the Day or Class

In my experience, if attendance is not done at the beginning of class, it is not done, or it is done late. In elementary schools, I have seen this routinely completed immediately after the students enter the classroom. A practical tip is to have students complete some type of morning activity while attendance is being taken. For example, in my son's kindergarten class, the teacher required all the students to "sign in," or print their name in a folder, and then put away their belongings while the teacher completed the attendance. At the secondary level, a warm-up activity to help the students focus immediately on the subject matter after entering the classroom is an effective way to start the class time and sets up the ideal time for teachers to take care of the attendance. In a high school English classroom that I have observed, the teacher takes attendance and then also has a student in the classroom record the absences and tardies for the day in the daily class log. This activity is assigned to a new student each day (see Resources for a Log Keeper sheet). This is extremely helpful for those who return from an absence to see who else was present on a particular day, and what assignments were missed. For attendance purposes, this also gives the teacher a back-up record of the class attendance, which can prove to be very helpful as suggested in this chapter.

Respond Immediately to Counselor or Administrative Summons

When classes are interrupted to summon students to the office, it is tempting to wait until a portion of the lesson is completed to release the student to the office. However, time often lapses, and the summons is forgotten. Meanwhile, someone in the front office is awaiting the teacher's response. This is an ideal example of how teachers should envision education as a collaborative and cooperative effort. Although teachers would like their classrooms to be left without interruptions, they must trust that these actions all contribute to the big picture that extends beyond the classroom. Cooperation is key here.

CONCLUSION

Besides preparing for their daily lessons, teachers must also make a myriad of decisions each day that regulate classroom routines and deal with the multiple clerical tasks involved in teaching. From assisting students who were absent with work they have missed to completing office paperwork promptly, teachers must have strategies in place for handling these numerous duties before they become overwhelming and too daunting for them to complete. By identifying and implementing practical tips for helping complete these procedural and managerial tasks efficiently, teachers will be able to carry out all these responsibilities while still preserving and maximizing instructional time in their classrooms.

৯ Practical Tips ৯

Procedural Tasks: Managing Daily Classroom Activities

- List the agenda and homework on the board.
- Create an Absent Folder for students to refer to on their own.
- Do not accept work that is late or e-mailed, but be sensitive to individual cases.
- Have a Weekly Work Folder.
- Have an emergency folder prepared for a substitute teacher.

Clerical Tasks: Managing Student Records and Completing Paperwork

- Ask parents when the best time is to reach them.
- Back up your attendance.
- Complete the lunch count with Popsicle sticks or clothespins.
- Keep a pen in your box.
- Complete attendance at the beginning of the day or class.
- Respond immediately to counselor or administrative summons.

CHAPTER FIVE

Discipline

Setting Boundaries and Holding the Line

Be bold in what you stand for and careful in what you fall for.

—Ruth Boorstin

C lassroom discipline is commonly cited as one of the most prevalent concerns that beginning teachers have. New teachers must set the boundaries for student behavior early on and communicate these standards clearly to the students. In addition, teachers must hold their line and not falter when reinforcing their expectations in the classroom. If teachers waver and release too much control to the students in the initial months of school, trying to regain control of their classroom afterward will be a weary and tiresome battle. The effects of this failure to reinforce one's discipline plan will appear throughout the school year, and classroom instruction will also be jeopardized. This chapter presents helpful insights into managing discipline successfully in the classroom.

YOU DON'T NEED FRIENDS— YOU NEED RESPECT

One important rule of thumb that teachers should remember before starting to teach is that they did not enter this profession simply to make friends with the students. Although it is human nature to want to be liked, simply coming across as a friendly, generous, or kindhearted leader at the beginning of the school year will most likely lead to difficulties with classroom discipline. What new teachers should remember is that they need to earn the respect of their students first, and then the admiration will follow. However, if a teacher sets out to be the students' friend at the beginning of the school year, students will more likely take advantage of the kindhearted tendencies of the teacher. This does not imply that teachers need to start off the year being mean, but they do need to be firm. If teachers are extremely firm at the outset, then there is still room to ease up as they get to know their students more personally throughout the school year. However, if teachers begin the school year with a low level of firmness and high levels of generosity and friendliness, then there is no room to release the reins in the classroom any more during the year without facing chaos and hardships. It is far more difficult to increase one's firmness and disciplinary tactics than to release them.

HAVE AN IMMEDIATE RESPONSE IN MIND TO ADDRESS DISAPPOINTING BEHAVIOR

One of the difficulties that beginning teachers face with discipline is exercising their authority and following through with consequences when a rule is broken or an expectation is not met. A helpful tip for new teachers is to create a phrase that they can use that quickly addresses a student's action and immediately expresses their disappointment with their behavior. In the past, I have used the phrase, "That behavior is inappropriate." Following my acknowledgment of the behavior, I would have a personal discussion with the student about the consequences merited for the behavior. Often, as a beginning teacher, I was either shocked by the behavior or simply did not have the words to respond right away to broken rules and unmet expectations. So I have found it helpful to have a short phrase in mind that can be used to acknowledge the behavior immediately.

One well-regarded high school English teacher requires her students to write letters of apology when any inappropriate actions occur in class. The behavior could have been a sarcastic comment, hurtful words, and unacceptable actions. The letter does not have to be long, and in fact, the ones that I have seen are usually just a few lines long. They have been addressed to the entire class or to an individual student. The exercise is effective because it helps students reflect on their inappropriate actions. I have also seen students call each other out on their poor behavior and tell one another that they owe someone a letter of apology. In this way, the students are self-regulating their own community and helping to manage the disciplinary measures in the class along with the teacher.

FIND WHAT MAKES STUDENTS TICK

Sometimes no matter what you do, a student may not be interested in the subject matter you are teaching and as a result can become unruly or disruptive in class. If students get to this point, it is helpful to discover where the root of their disruption stems from and learn what makes them tick or motivates them to do better. For instance, at the secondary level, some students are motivated by sports programs, so working with their coaches is an effective way to help shape their behavior more positively in class. At the elementary level, teachers should talk to the parents or caregivers to see what personal interests or passions the students have. Afterward, a behavior contract or motivational plan can be constructed that includes the information learned about what makes them tick in the classroom. The praise of a student's coach or the incentive to do well in class to attain a reward that involves the student's passion or interest is a method that can be used as motivation. For example, if a student enjoys a particular type of music, then the teacher might play that music during class as a reward to the student for having accomplished a particular goal. Parents and teachers can also team up to create appropriate incentives and rewards to motivate students.

MAP OUT SMALL GOALS TO HELP STRUGGLING STUDENTS MAKE BABY STEPS: CONTINGENCY CONTRACTS

Some students can become easily overwhelmed with large tasks and become disruptive or lose focus quickly. For these students, small goals need to be mapped out, and contingency contracts can be drawn up so that students are rewarded for their baby steps and kept on task. At the elementary level, this may mean that a small notecard with a few boxes drawn on it is taped to the student's desk. When the student finishes one task, he or she will be given a sticker or stamp to note the accomplished goal. Once all the boxes are filled, the student can be rewarded with a special prize or privilege, such as eating lunch with the teacher or picking a prize from a treasure chest. The idea here is that the student remains engaged and on task rather than left to struggle and become disruptive in the classroom. At the secondary level, students, parents, coaches, and counselors can all be involved in creating the contingency contracts and negotiating the rewards.

PARTNER UP AND PLAY FISH OUT OF WATER

I have had a few secondary students during my career who simply chose not to learn or work in my class. I shared my frustrations with a colleague, and we discovered that we both had students in our classrooms at the same time who were not participating and whose negative energy was not helping the others in our class. So my colleague and I partnered up and played "fish out of water." We warned each other when we might send over our apathetic students to each other's classrooms with a work assignment that was required to be completed by the end of the class period. The student spent the class period in another classroom with the students asking why the student was not in his or her own classroom. This was usually enough to make the student feel uncomfortable, and soon thereafter, the student's behavior usually improved.

COMMUNICATE WITH ADMINISTRATION

When discipline issues associated with a particular student had consumed my thoughts and my energy, I would communicate this with my department or grade level chairperson or one of the administrative leaders at my school. It is difficult to anticipate what might happen at any given time with students who are creating disciplinary problems in the classroom. Even if the problems have been handled and taken care of between the teacher and the student, it is best to document the behavior by sharing the events with the administration. In this way, should questions arise, or should others mention the incident to the principal or chairperson, they will be well informed of the situation.

USE E-MAIL TO DOCUMENT EVIDENCE OF DISCIPLINARY ACTIONS

A colleague once pointed out to me that the *E* in e-mail stands for evidence. So, using e-mail as a source of evidence as well as a communication tool is an effective way to document discipline in a classroom. If numerous e-mails have been exchanged between parents and school personnel regarding a particular student, then the e-mails can be filed in one folder on a teacher's computer and easily accessed by the teacher. This method of documentation also saves the teacher time because separate notes may not have to be written for the parents and the administrator to document the disciplinary action. Using e-mail can be a helpful tool when documenting and managing the disciplinary issues in one's classroom.

DETENTION DOES NOT EQUAL FUN: GIVE THEM SOMETHING TO DO

When I taught high school classes, one of the first consequences in my class for inappropriate behavior was detention with me in my classroom. Once a boy came to serve his detention, and he sat down and talked to me the whole time. In my mind, his detention was his punishment because he could not be with his friends or do other things with his time. However, at the end of his detention, he said that he enjoyed talking to me so much that he would like to have detention again. This really made me think. I had an endless list of tasks that needed to be completed, and I had someone who could help me with it, but instead, he just sat through his detention and watched me frantically try to check off more on my to-do list. I realized that if students serve detention I would have them work on something constructive for me, such as filing student work, cleaning desks, scraping gum off the bottom of the desks, erasing the board, or cleaning my windows. After that, detention with me was not as much fun for my students.

GIVE AFFIRMATIVE COMMANDS
RATHER THAN NEGATIVE ONES

In a classroom setting, it is easy to tell students what they cannot do: "Don't chew gum. Don't talk when I'm talking. Don't cheat." However, teachers should try to use affirmative commands, rather than starting their commands off with "don't." Students can tune out the rest of the sentence when it begins with a negative word like *don't*. So, think of spinning expectations positively in the classroom by using affirmative commands such as, "Throw out your gum. Pay attention to these important announcements. Do your own work." It is good to put a positive spin on things when possible.

ENCOURAGE STUDENTS
WHENEVER POSSIBLE

In terms of disciplinary issues, it seems logical to assume that students who misbehave or those who do not stay on task should be punished in some way and then redirected. However, rather than resorting to punishment as the first line of defense, teachers should consider using praise or encouragement to help shape student behavior. Students might be pleasantly surprised by a teacher who holds them accountable through positive words and who challenges them to set and meet a higher standard for themselves. Some students may just need to hear that someone believes in them, has faith that they are capable of doing more, and will hold them accountable to do just that. In addition, praising students for their appropriate behavior and recognizing the exceptional models in class present visual examples of behavior for all to follow. For example, holding up a student's work and affirming his or her efforts and work completed in class or complimenting a particular student for noteworthy behavior positively reinforces the student and helps the other students view a model of good work or helpful actions. Encouraging students whenever possible promotes positive teaching and learning and helps to deal with disciplinary matters in a constructive way.

BE MINDFUL OF YOUR INVISIBLE DISCIPLINE METHODS: YOUR REPUTATION

A teacher's disciplinary methods involve more than punishments and rewards. Teachers should realize that their classroom management skills, their attention to detail, their professionalism, excellent teaching, creativity, and organization all contribute to the success of their disciplinary plans for their classrooms. Students recognize the efforts of hardworking, innovative, and conscientious teachers, and these strong work ethics and high standards that teachers uphold are rewarded by the respect that students show for these types of teachers. In a practical sense, students appreciate teachers who return papers promptly, who manage instructional time effectively, and who are good teachers. Those who are committed to and carry out good teaching in their classrooms will produce well-disciplined classrooms. Students will defend and praise good teachers both in and outside the classroom, and soon disciplinary problems are minimized not only because of the efforts of the teacher but those of the students as well.

CONCLUSION

Classroom discipline may be a difficult task, but it is a critical element to achieving success in teaching. Although it may be a traditional practice to use punishment as a disciplinary measure, many other practical options should be considered to maintain discipline in one's classroom. Carrying out a high standard for consistent, effective instruction is one of the key ways of setting the stage for good discipline in one's classroom. Students will respect and honor those teachers who are committed to good teaching and demonstrate respect for both whom they teach and what they teach. Last, the tactics for effective classroom discipline are not limited only to the tips listed in this chapter; rather, successful classroom discipline is strongly related to paying careful attention to the interdependent factors of teaching that are presented in all the chapters of this book.

&ro; Practical Tips &rs;

- You don't need friends—You need respect.
- Have an immediate response in mind to address disappointing behavior.
- Find what makes students tick.
- Map out small goals to help struggling students make baby steps: Contingency contracts.
- Partner up and play fish out of water.
- Communicate with administration.
- Use e-mail as evidence of disciplinary actions.
- Detention does not equal fun; give them something to do.
- Give affirmative commands rather than negative ones.
- Encourage students whenever possible.
- Be mindful of your invisible discipline methods: your reputation.

PART III

Instructional Strategies

CHAPTER SIX

Teaching
Outside the Box

*Remember: A student's greatest thinking will come from his
or her ability to break away—not to conform.*

—Author Unknown

O ne of the greatest challenges that teachers face is accommo-
dating the needs of all students. Classrooms are filled with
students with various types of talents and abilities. For instance,
some students' strengths may lie in auditory processing, whereas
others may need to kinesthetically process their learning. Given
the multiple ways that students learn, lesson plans using traditional teaching strategies that incorporate a "one recipe for all"
method of teaching are not likely to ensure success for all students.
For example, not all students learn their spelling words after having written each of them three times. Also, in the same way, not
all students learn their vocabulary words from their foreign language class by just writing the word and its translation on a sheet
of paper. Varied instructional practices and "thinking outside the
box" of traditional learning practices are needed in today's classrooms. New teachers, who are struggling through the survival
stages of the early years of teaching, may be tempted to resort to

traditional teaching methods; however, this pedagogy does not address the individual needs of all students. More specifically, students with special needs and their parents may become easily disgruntled and frustrated with the traditional teaching and learning process. Although certain teaching methodologies have been used for years and are readily available to new teachers from their own memories and experiences, this tendency to resort to "what worked for us" may set a trap of sticking to particular teaching strategies that in reality are not effective. Some teachers believe that they are not creative enough to think outside the box on their own, and for these reasons, this chapter is dedicated to sharing some creative teaching strategies that will help to reach all students.

THE BEHAVIORAL DOMAIN: GUIDE STUDENTS' LEARNING

Redirect Students With Special Needs

For students with special needs, learning needs to be broken up into small chunks of time, and praise plays a large role in keeping the student on task and motivated. Integrating tasks that involve sensorimotor skills for these students is a helpful way to keep them engaged in learning. For example, after a student completes a chunk of learning, the teacher may redirect his or her energy to another task as a reward. The student may take some books back to the school library, run a message to the administrative offices, or complete another clerical task in the room. This redirection benefits students with special needs and helps manage their behavior constructively in the learning process.

Scaffold Videos

Videos can be helpful educational tools, but often they are not presented effectively to maximize the learning that can be associated with this teaching technique. Students have associated videos with "a day off," and this should not be the case. If the use of videos in a classroom is not presented effectively, a teacher's management of student behavior in the classroom for that day may go awry. Teachers should introduce the lesson and the video by stating the objective for watching the video, and then a worksheet, notes, or some other type of scaffold should be provided so that the students remain focused during the video and understand why they are spending their class time watching it. Scaffolding videos helps to manage student behavior during these special lessons and supports the learning that is intended during these activities.

MAP It Out

Students need to be taught how to organize their time and manage it successfully. With extracurricular activities and family responsibilities competing for students' time after school, it is easy for students to become distracted and overwhelmed. Often, students do not know how to manage their time efficiently in order to complete their academic responsibilities at home. Helping students to map out how their time after school will be used is helpful.

The acronym MAP stands for mandatory, additional, prize. The first category, *mandatory* (M), should include a list of the items that the students must complete that evening. If the assignment is due the next day of school, then that task should be written under this category. Writing these tasks down on paper is a powerful exercise for students because the list will present a tangible and visual representation of what needs to be completed. It brings forth these prioritized items from the invisible world to the visible world.

Next, students may list items in the *additional* (A) category that they would like to complete that evening simply so that they may work ahead. In this case, if an assignment is not due for a few days but students want to complete some research or other work for the assignment, they may choose to use their remaining time on these tasks.

Finally, if the mandatory (M) category items and the additional (A) category items have been completed, then students can treat themselves to a special reward from the *prize* (P) category. This prize may involve spending time with a friend, watching television, or attending an event. Parents could require that students have their MAPs signed by their teachers, and teachers could assign MAPs to their classes as a daily exercise that teaches responsibility and efficient time-management techniques.

Teachers might also consider filling out a MAP to help manage their time after school. It is easy to feel overwhelmed with the numerous responsibilities of teaching, which include but are not limited to lesson planning, grading, reading, and attending students' activities. These professional tasks, combined with personal responsibilities at home, can leave teachers crazed as they try to accomplish too many things at once and end up not being able to accomplish the tasks that should have taken priority—those that need to be completed before the next day. Teachers as well as students need to MAP out their day's tasks so that the items that should be completed right away actually do get done first.

THE COGNITIVE DOMAIN: INCORPORATE BRAIN-DIFFERENTIATED LEARNING

This next section presents tips and insights into how teachers can vary the methodologies that are involved in the cognitive processes of teaching and learning. These ideas are examples of how teachers can think outside the box and achieve successful learning outcomes. The theoretical foundation of these strategies lies in brain-differentiated learning principles. Recent research about learning styles and the brain (Jensen, 1995, 2000, 2001; Sousa, 2001; Sylwester, 1995; Tate, 2003; Wolfe, 2001) has identified a variety of teaching strategies that take advantage of how brains learn best. This section showcases how these strategies have been carried out in some of today's classrooms.

Vary Your Lesson Plans

There are definitely days when formulated or prefabricated lesson plans may be necessary, but sticking to the same format for teaching will quickly bore the students and put teachers in the categories of ordinary and typical. Students appreciate teachers who vary lesson plan structures and incorporate different teaching strategies. I remember a student in my secondary classroom once said, "I love this class because we always do something different." Some days we moved our desks into big circles to have large class discussions, and other days I threw big blankets on the floor and brought in milk and cookies while we read our Spanish literature on the floor. Changing the traditional lesson plan is a detail that will not go unnoticed.

In my son's fifth grade classroom, the teacher motivates the students to complete their homework all week by offering the reward of "Fun Fridays." If the students turn in their homework consistently all week, then the teacher presents a "fun" lesson for them on Fridays. For instance, one Friday, the students took magnifying glasses outside and tried to roast marshmallows using the sun's rays and a magnifying glass. Another Fun Friday involved making ice cream. Having some type of fun project motivated the students to get their homework done, and the teacher's efforts to vary the instruction and offer something out of the ordinary for Fridays will leave a memorable impression on the hearts and minds of her fifth graders.

Individualize Instruction

Being fair does not always mean treating everyone equally. Students all bring something different to learning, and therefore, teachers might often find themselves in a place where they can modify the teaching and learning for a particular student. Individualizing instruction can highlight students' strengths, lift their self-esteem, and ensure their success. For the student who has difficulty with writing, have him or her recite more of the oral prompts for the Spanish final, rather than writing out the mini-composition. Or, have the elementary student who struggles with writing out entire sentences for dictation just write out the spelling words. Another suggestion might be to have the student do the even numbers on the math assignment rather than the whole assignment. Learning centers in elementary classrooms could also be geared to the strengths of students with special needs. If a teacher has assessed that certain students are particularly gifted in art or logic, then the learning centers could incorporate special art projects or challenging logic puzzles. Students could then be encouraged to attend the learning centers around the room that give them the opportunities to exercise their strengths. Individualizing instruction and helping students with special needs know that you care enough to modify your plans will increase the students' respect for you as a teacher and decrease your disciplinary problems.

Incorporate Brain Strategies: The Three P's: Positive, Purpose, Primacy-Recency

One effective way to manage a classroom is to incorporate strategies that are correlated with brain research and varied learning theories. Using the 20 strategies identified in *Worksheets Don't Grow Dendrites: 20 Instructional Strategies That Engage the Brain* (Tate, 2003) to help engage students, make learning fun, and manage a classroom successfully. Here are just three tips that should be remembered when managing your classroom:

1. Start Your Class Off With Something POSITIVE

Brain research has shown that positive interactions not only create a positive learning environment, but they also start the lesson by getting the full attention of the learner (Tate, 2003). The student's body language, attentiveness, and motivation to learn are heightened when the brain is engaged in something positive. Starting class off with something positive is an effective management tool that should be used to grab the students' attention easily and to start the lesson with the maximum potential for learning.

2. Communicate Your PURPOSE

Students like structure, and they want to know what to expect in schools. Stating the purpose of any lesson communicates clearly to students the goals that they will accomplish during the given class period, the expectation for their engagement in class and the purpose of the time spent together is understood, and class time begins with a focused goal.

3. Practice the PRIMACY-RECENCY Principle

The primacy-recency principle states that the top two items that a brain remembers best in a lesson are the first thing it hears (primacy) and the last thing it hears (recency). Tate (2004) recommends that teachers open their lessons with a strong introduction and then close their teaching with a memorable segment. By beginning class with thought-provoking or interesting material, teachers will engage their audience quickly. Making sure to cover key points in the end will sear the main points of the lesson into the students' memories and will help students to retain and retrieve knowledge more effectively. The closure is a critical step that is often missing in lesson plans. Teachers commonly mistake cleaning up and collecting supplies after a lesson as the closure, but the concluding step should be the repetition or recitation of the objectives of the day's lessons—that is what the students should leave remembering. Incorporating the primacy-recency principle into one's teaching will help structure the class and its contents in an effective, logical, and powerful manner.

Incorporating brain strategies like the three P's, Positive, Purpose, and Primacy-Recency, helps set a positive tone, an organized structure, and an effective learning environment for classrooms. Students appreciate cohesive, structured classrooms where lessons are carefully organized and presented in a positive way. When students are motivated to learn and when they respect the classroom and the teacher, discipline issues are also minimized. These elements will all contribute to managing one's classroom more smoothly and effectively.

ELEMENTARY: SPELLING IDEAS

Don't Just Write Spelling Words Down on Paper

When we think back to how we learned spelling words, most of us can recall the exercise where we were asked to write the words three or more times on a piece of paper. However, using this traditional method to reinforce spelling does not connect with the many diverse learning modalities that students possess. This section provides creative methods that teachers could easily implement.

Use Sidewalk Chalk

Students could go out to the playground and write the words on the blacktop. For homework or extra credit, students could be encouraged to write their spelling words around their neighborhoods and on their driveways or sidewalks. This learning activity promotes socially constructed learning through the student's interaction with adults, as well as kinesthetic learning from moving around and incorporating the novel method of learning spelling words outside using sidewalk chalk. Also, this activity is much more fun than being inside with the traditional paper and pen.

Write Letters on Clothespins

Have students pin up their spelling words on a clothesline. Teachers can carry out this activity as a learning center in a classroom, encourage students to use it as a method to help reinforce spelling at home. Another idea is to write words on balloons. When the students know how to spell the words, then they can pop the balloons or make a balloon bouquet.

Sponge-Paint the Words and Hang Them Up for Everyone to See

This fun activity and the visuals that it produces will have students continually looking at their spelling words.

Sing the Words Into a Tape Recorder

Have students sing the spelling words into a tape recorder and then play the recording each morning as students enter the classroom. Students can sing along to the tape, and through the repetition and use of music and rhythm, the spelling words will be reinforced in an enjoyable way.

Use Shaving Cream

Spray some shaving cream on the students' desks and let them spell the words out in the shaving cream. This activity will clean their desks and help them to learn their spelling words in an unforgettable way.

Scratch Each Other's Backs With the Letters

This activity can be carried out in a number of ways. For example, the teacher could ask one student to come to the front of the room and have students watch while she traces a spelling word on a student's back; the volunteer or a student in the audience could guess the spelling word. Parents could also be encouraged to use this technique at home.

Shape Letters With Your Body

Spelling out the words with students' bodies is a kinesthetic activity that gets the kids moving and engaged in an amusing and interactive method to help learn their spelling words. Students can also dance to their recording of the spelling words. Dance moves that represent the letters of the words are fun to create and are a very helpful way to learn kinesthetically.

ELEMENTARY: MATH IDEAS

Play Multiplication Twister

Students can learn and practice their multiplication facts using the game of Twister. Multiplication equations are written down on flashcards, and the answers to the equations are written on or taped to the various colored dots of a Twister Board. Each student must answer the multiplication equation by reaching for the answers that are on the Twister Board. Continue with more equations until one of the students falls. This interactive, humorous, and fun method of learning will help students to practice their math facts and remember them for a long time.

Do the Hustle

One of the most creative ways that I have ever seen the number line concept introduced was with the Number Line Hustle. Tate (2003) has students visualize that they are on the midpoint, or zero, of a number line and then plays the song, "The Hustle." She calls out an algebraic equation such as, "5 + (−3) equals," and students begin by taking 5 steps to the right, and then coming back 3 steps to the left, and finally finding themselves at the number 2 on the number line. This exercise of visualization and body movement helps to reinforce this basic math concept.

ELEMENTARY: SCIENCE

Act Out Landforms

Have students act out earth's landforms. For example, students can stand up and raise their hands to a point in the air to become the Rocky Mountains. To represent a desert, they stand like a cactus and flash ten fingers to let the teacher know that a desert receives less than 10 inches of precipitation a year. To make a plateau, students use a partner and connect one hand to the other person's head making a flattop. A basin is acted out by having students make a bowl with their hands and pretending to eat cereal. These active methods of teaching will sear the definitions of landforms into the long-term memories of the students.

SECONDARY STRATEGIES

As students become older and more independent, it seems that teaching methods typically become less varied and rely more upon the basic skills of listening comprehension through lecture and solid note-taking. Yet there are many ways that secondary teachers can think outside the box when teaching academic concepts in their classrooms. Here are some examples.

Paint

Although painting is a common practice in elementary schools, it is commonly left out in secondary classrooms. But students are attracted to this method of learning and intrigued by its novelty at this stage of education. I have seen students paint math concepts that they are learning and hang them up in their classrooms. In my own teaching, I have had students finger-paint words in Spanish when they are learning the rules for spelling changes of special verbs. Painting the letters, remembering that they have special spelling rules, and even choosing specific colors to note the significance of the letters or rule that needs to be remembered are all creative ways to use paint.

Use Music, Rhythm, Rhyme, and Rap

One of my favorite brain-differentiated learning strategies from Tate's *20 Instructional Strategies That Engage the Brain* (2003) is incorporating music, rhythm, rhyme, and rap in classrooms. One master teacher that I have worked with made up a rap to teach his students what anonymous meant: "Anonymous—unsigned; written by a person whose name is unknown," they sang as they clapped and chanted to a beat while reinforcing the word's definition throughout the class period. If teachers don't feel that they are creative enough to make up their own musical piece, then they can ask the students to create an original piece of their own. History teachers could create raps as Clark did in his book *The Excellent 11* (2004), to teach students about the United States' presidents and their legacies. Classical background music is also helpful. It can mask other, more distracting noises from the environment and helps set a pleasant mood during writing activities such as journaling.

Use Role-Play

This technique is an effective method for having students visualize and act out the roles of the people they are studying. History classes are prime environments for such methods to be implemented. I have seen students sit on the floor and gather around an artificial fire, pretending they are American Indians having a powwow and discussing what their plans should be when the white men come to take over their land. Another example of role-playing carried out in a history classroom is to have students who are studying about slavery huddle under their desks and pretend that the small space they are huddled under is the slave ship, while listening to tapes of former slaves telling their stories.

Teachers can also take up role-playing in their classrooms. In my Spanish classes, I dressed up as different Spanish-speaking characters, such as Sor Juana Inés de la Cruz and Benito Juarez, and began my class pretending I was this prominent figure. Every student left the classroom knowing some key facts about each historical figure and remembering this lesson. Role-playing is a powerful teaching tool.

Don't Just Test Them

At the secondary level, written testing is a common way to formally assess student learning. However, when other nontraditional forms of assessment are used, students can learn more from the process, and teachers can see the breadth and depth of their students' learning. So, when it is possible, instead of simply giving students a written test at the end of a unit, teachers should be encouraged to think outside the box and give students a choice in their assessment. The students could create a short video production, an original Web-based activity like Webquest that others could use, an artistic work with an accompanying explanation, or other creative work that demonstrates their understanding of the material. I am confident that both the students and the teachers will be amazed at the end products. The learning that is assessed and accomplished by breaking out of the box of formal testing will be surprising and impressive.

CONCLUSION

Classrooms are filled with students with varied learning abilities. As teachers, we should be committed to varying our instruction so that learning can be maximized for all students in our classrooms. Although the rigorous demands of the teaching profession can quickly extinguish the energy of new teachers, this chapter has offered some examples of how teachers continue to press on and to think outside the box. All of these strategies do not necessarily require extra time for preparation on the teacher's part, but they do require teachers to have a vision that moves them beyond the traditional schemata of classroom teaching. By investing in this vision and sharing these innovative strategies amongst one another in the teaching profession, teaching can be raised to an exciting new level for all who are involved.

✍ Practical Tips ✍

- Redirect students with special needs.
- Scaffold videos.
- MAP it out.
- Vary lesson plans.
- Individualize instruction.
- Incorporate brain-differentiated learning strategies.
  - Start class off with something positive.
  - Communicate your purpose.
  - Practice the primacy-recency principle.

- Elementary spelling ideas:
  - Don't just write spelling words down on paper.
  - Use sidewalk chalk.
  - Write letters on clothespins.
  - Sponge-paint the words and hang them up for everyone to see.
  - Sing the words into a tape recorder.
  - Use shaving cream.
  - Scratch each other's backs with the letters.
  - Shape letters with your body.

- Elementary math ideas
  - Make up a game like Multiplication Twister.
  - Do the hustle.

- Elementary science ideas
  - Act out landforms.

- Secondary strategies
  - Paint.
  - Use music, rhythm, rhyme, and rap.
  - Use role-play.
  - Don't just test them.

CHAPTER SEVEN

A Personal Touch

Incorporating the "Affective" Element

Excellence is to do a common thing in an uncommon way.

—Booker T. Washington

I have observed, interacted with, and known many teachers over the years, and as I reflect on the attributes of exceptional teachers, it has become clear to me that they all pay careful attention to incorporating affective elements into their teaching. Well-regarded teachers, or those whom we recognize as having made an eternal impact on our lives, have risen to the top because they have done something extra to set them apart from the majority. These are the personal details that make them unique and unforgettable. Many of these ideas focus on students' self-esteem and motivation. Teachers' common responses and expectations impact students negatively if students simply do not possess the abilities to accomplish certain academic tasks. As a result, teachers should consider the following strategies so that they can partner alongside their students in the journey of learning.

PROTECT AND NURTURE THE
SELF-ESTEEM OF STUDENTS

Students with special needs in particular can easily enter a downward spiral that leads to negative self-esteem if they are continually unable to meet the expectations of a regular classroom. A plethora of "no's," red pen markings, and time spent after school or during recess to complete work can quickly add more tension and pain for students who have difficulty learning. One parent commented that her daughter who suffered from attention-deficit disorder felt that her teachers were "beating her up." Some students may always need extra time to complete tasks, or they may not have the resources necessary to complete what teachers believe is a simple task. Continuing to punish these students by taking away privileges will do more harm than many teachers realize.

When a student with special needs is not able to release his or her energy at recess or has to remain in class to finish work, the struggle to complete tasks often becomes greater and greater throughout the day. The student may end up feeling defeated and overwhelmed in the classroom. Finding a learning outcome compromise to suit the capabilities of individual students and protecting and nurturing their self-esteem are of paramount importance. Some methods that teachers should consider are using a different color correction pen, making sure to add positive comments as well as constructive ones, and allowing students to go to recess or not to have to stay after school even though an entire assignment is not completed. Making these compromises and understanding the special needs of students play a powerful role in the teaching and learning process.

ATTEND SCHOOL ACTIVITIES

Attending school activities at both the elementary and secondary levels demonstrates a teacher's personal investment in their students' interests outside the classroom and makes an indescribable difference in a teacher's reputation and classroom management. Being at the musicals, fundraisers, and special events does make a difference in your teaching and also makes a notable impression on the students. Elementary school students are in awe when they see their teachers outside the classroom, and seeing this other dimension of their teachers seems to garner more respect and admiration from their young students. At the secondary level, attending athletic events, chaperoning dances, and supporting the students in their extracurricular activities play a significant role in teaching. Students appreciate the extra efforts that teachers make to be involved in student life, and that involvement also opens up other opportunities for personal conversations of special interest. This is how teachers can personally invest in their students' lives, which in turn builds relationships and promotes a mutual respect between students and teachers both inside and outside the classroom.

REWARD STUDENTS FOR MEETING SHORT-TERM GOALS

Completing a long assignment may seem overwhelming for some students. At the elementary levels, this type of assignment may involve a task such as writing spelling sentences, whereas at the secondary levels this is best exemplified by writing an essay. At both the elementary and secondary levels, the content area of mathematics offers the example of the daunting task of completing one page of approximately 30 problems from a textbook. Such tasks involve long periods of concentration, and this is more challenging for some students than others.

One way that teachers could help students so that they do not feel as overwhelmed with long assignments is to reward them for short-term goals that will help students eventually to complete the long-term goal. If students must write 20 spelling sentences, have them stand after completing 7 sentences and do a little dance while playing a quick, upbeat song. Then, offer another incentive at the 14-sentence mark. Creating short-term goals like this may also apply for a math assignment. Once students hit the 5-problem mark, offer them a fun reward. For students who are writing an essay, reward them for brainstorming the content of their writing by offering a reward. The rewards can vary from candy to dances, to special songs played while writing, to a silly act carried out by the teacher in class. (Students love to see their teachers being silly!) The students should have choices with the rewards. Be creative!

A "wheel of fortune" that offers various awards could be made and spun by a student after he or she reaches a short-term goal. The point is that breaking learning up into smaller chunks positively affects the students' outlook on accomplishing a task, making it more likely that all students will attain success.

REMEMBER BIRTHDAYS

At both the elementary and secondary levels, students' birthdays should not be overlooked. Every child, if not person, likes to feel appreciated and special on his or her birthday. Some may not get this special attention at home, so it is a special detail that could be generously extended by a teacher that may leave an unforgettable impression on a student. At the elementary levels, students may wear special birthday crowns and enjoy delicious birthday treats that are donated by the families or the teacher. Teachers might even extend a free homework pass or special privilege for the day. At the secondary level, teachers should not be fooled into thinking that students are too old to appreciate little details like birthday certificates, stickers, birthday pencils, free homework passes, the singing or playing of a special birthday song, or a special treat. Even students at this age appreciate the attention that teachers pay to these details. One high school teacher whom I have observed writes a special birthday greeting on her board, and then the birthday student gets to pick a special song to be played during class from the teacher's music selection (i.e., Stevie Wonder's "Happy Birthday" or the Beatles' "Birthday"). For elementary-age students, the teacher could also help the student feel special by placing a birthday "trophy" or small stuffed animal on the student's desk. At any age, remembering someone's birthday is a detail that is always appreciated.

USE SNACKS AS REWARDS AND INCENTIVES

Food brings out a positive emotion in us all. Perhaps it is the novelty of including food in our classrooms that gets students all excited or motivates them in an inexplicable way, but using snacks as rewards or incentives is a detail that usually produces positive results. I also believe that sharing in some type of food together as a class builds community. It is a traditional ritual that people gather together to share food, enjoy conversation, and build relationships.

Incorporating this detail into one's teaching does not mean that teachers must be responsible for paying for the food. Students can contribute to this element of your class. For instance, for special class parties, students or homeroom parents can each sign up to contribute an item to the party. At the elementary level, asking one to three families to contribute a beverage or food item should cover the whole class. At the secondary level, each student can contribute a snack, paper plates and napkins, or beverage. If items are left over, then an incentive can be presented to enjoy the leftovers at a later time. Teachers should, however, learn the health issues of their students and be particularly attentive to special food allergies. These precautions should be communicated to the families who are donating food items. Another suggestion is to have the students with special food allergies have a box of treats sent in at the beginning of the semester from which they can select an item during these special occasions.

Incorporating food into one's classroom successfully can set the stage for community building, which contributes to a positive and motivating classroom environment. One time I had a student at the secondary level who forgot to bring in the brownies that he volunteered to bring for our class party. The class was small and very close-knit, and they felt comfortable teasing him about forgetting the brownies, because he had teased others in the past for forgetting their treats. His mother happened to be on our high school staff, and one Thursday, she randomly came by at the beginning of our class to drop off enough brownies and milk for the whole class. Soon after, we called Thursdays "Brownie Thursday" because the students had formulated a rotating list of people who were responsible for bringing in brownies and milk every Thursday after that. The students enjoyed the snack quietly and happily while we completed our warm-up exercises. This little detail, "Brownie Thursdays," built a sense of community within our classroom, did not interrupt or take away from instruction, and to this day when I see those students, they recall this memory that we built together. More than just the food, I am convinced that the camaraderie and community that we shared set that class apart from many others in their high school careers.

USE MUSIC AS AN AFFECTIVE TOOL IN THE CLASSROOM

Music is a powerful tool in the classroom. Recent studies on the brain and memory found that music is a powerful carrier of signals that activate emotion and long-term memory (Tate, 2004). The selection of music can set the stage and determine the tone or rhythm of a lesson or class period. Playing upbeat music when students enter the room can bring smiles to faces and a positive beginning to class. Instrumental or classical pieces can set the stage for journal writing, and a wide range of emotions can be invoked through various genres of music. I can still recall perfectly the day that I incorporated music into my secondary Spanish classroom. My students reacted positively to an upbeat Latin rhythm that I played while they entered the classroom. Their attitudes changed that day, and I firmly believe that my struggles as a beginning teacher with classroom management and discipline significantly improved after that day. In the same way, at the elementary level, using music to learn content has been proven to be very helpful. Jensen (2001) found that music activates and synchronizes neural networks that increase the brain's ability to reason spatially and think creatively. I also observed a middle school teacher who taught her students songs to help aid classroom management issues such as passing in papers. Students passed in papers while singing songs like "Yellow Submarine." At the end of the song, all the papers were collected and put in their place—a perfect management tool. In the same way, students at the elementary level know that it is time to clean up when the teacher plays a "clean-up song" while they are putting things back in their place. So, music can be used as a tool to increase learning and manage one's classroom.

WRITE ENCOURAGING NOTES TO STUDENTS

Everyone could have a bad day, or could just be going through the motions of daily life without any encouraging words. Often, when I saw that a particular student seemed down or discouraged, I would take a quick minute to write a note of encouragement to bring a little sunshine to his or her day. When the student was not looking, I left the Post-it or small note on top of the student's desk or backpack with a small treat, like a lollipop or fun pencil. Notes such as "Believe in yourself: I appreciate your efforts in my class" are much appreciated and may make all the difference in your relationship with a particular student. Having a bag full of small treats and notes handy is a small detail that adds a personal and caring side to your teaching.

SHARE COMPLIMENTS AND PRAISE STUDENTS IN CLASS

Besides writing notes to compliment and praise your students, affirming students aloud in class is another detail that students appreciate. A student's self-esteem rises with compliments and praise from the teacher, and these exceptionally recognized behaviors also provide examples for the other students to follow. At the secondary level, it is also fascinating to see the ripple effect after praising particular students. The students leave your class and tell their friends that you praised a particular student, and soon the compliment has rippled into many circles of friends, and the teacher's one compliment has magnified. Sharing compliments and praising your students promotes positive self-esteem in students and in your classroom.

BE SOMEONE'S CHEERLEADER

Having worked with students at all levels and studied various aspects of the teaching and learning process, I am convinced that one of the fundamental details that leads to success in teaching is simply to invest personally in the lives of the students, and to be someone's cheerleader. We all need someone in our corner; someone to tell us that he or she believes in us, that we should believe in ourselves, and that we can rise above the obstacles set before us. We are all capable of learning something, but we may learn a little more with someone on our side to inspire us along the way. Although it may be difficult to invest personally in all of them, teachers might recognize the special needs of even just a few students, whom they will teach and mentor beyond the walls of a classroom.

As human beings, we like to feel—and very well may need to be—validated. There is power in the positive energy that is formed in knowing that we are valued. Finding something that is valuable in each of our students and praising them for their gifts, talents, and achievements play an important role in the teaching and learning process. Attending students' athletic events, highlighting a "student of the week," asking about their extracurricular activities, and being their cheerleaders whenever we can—these details all add a magical component to the teaching profession. Everyone needs a cheerleader. When students reflect back on their teachers, they will not remember each lesson that was taught and each standard that was met, but they will remember if a teacher invested in their life in some personal way. Celebrating the person, the spirit of each student, and partnering in the journey of learning with each individual reap indescribable fruit, which is the reason, I believe, that teachers keep teaching.

CONCLUSION

A typical classroom experience is commonly associated with the following components: (a) a teacher-directed lesson, (b) students' desks that are carefully aligned in rows, (c) students who are intently listening to a lecture, and (d) homework that is assigned to reinforce the lesson's objective. Although this may be the regularly accepted format for teaching, incorporating the personal details outlined in this chapter into one's teaching disbands the expectation or schema that we have of ordinary teaching. Both students and parents appreciate these special efforts that create a climate for endless possibilities in creative, effective, and successful teaching.

❧ Practical Tips ❦

- Protect and nurture the self-esteem of students.
- Attend school activities.
- Reward students for meeting short-term goals.
- Remember birthdays.
- Use snacks as rewards and incentives.
- Use music as an "affective" tool in the classroom.
- Write encouraging notes to students.
- Share compliments and praise students in class.
- Be someone's cheerleader.

PART IV
Teaching: An Ensemble Work

CHAPTER EIGHT

Cooperate, Collaborate, and Consider the Office Staff

Never doubt that a small group of thoughtful, committed people can change the world. Indeed, it is the only thing that ever has.

—Margaret Mead

The teaching profession can be isolating because teachers spend the majority of their workdays in their classrooms, separated from their colleagues. However, working alone all the time is not helpful to a teacher's emotional well-being or professional growth. Teachers must make efforts to move outside their classrooms during their prep periods, lunch, or after school so that collegial relationships are fostered. Teachers who contribute to and invest in their school's community will maximize their potential pool of resources and strengthen the connections that are needed to regulate school procedures and teach. Just as it takes many bodily systems functioning together for the human body to thrive, it takes the cooperation and communication of the various departments of teachers and staff of a school to help teachers thrive in a classroom. This chapter presents suggestions for how teachers can cooperate and collaborate with one another and with the office staff so that teaching can be viewed as a shared, communal effort.

ACKNOWLEDGE THE STAFF AS PART OF THE TEAM

Given that much of teachers' daily activities involve the office staff, an essential lesson for all teachers to learn is to work cooperatively with the staff and to consider them equal contributors in the educational enterprise. During my initial visit to my first teaching job in a high school, I walked into the front office and encountered a group of women all sitting in a circle in the main office eating their lunches. Although I did not know any one of them then, I reflect back on my teaching career and cannot imagine functioning, let alone succeeding as a teacher, without them. This important ring of leaders consisted of the office manager, the attendance manager, the assistant to the athletics director, a guidance counselor, the librarian, the nurse, and others from the front office staff. These staff members all played an important role in my work with students—from the daily procedures of managing attendance records to counseling students through the sensitive issues of divorce or deaths in their families. Together, we served the students, and it is important to respect their work by promptly responding to their requests and returning their paperwork. Unfortunately, I have often sensed a hierarchy at schools regarding the teachers and the office staff, and this division can threaten the sense of community that is needed in schools. When any part of a school, whether it is the office staff, a particular department, or the administration, believes that their work is more important than another, this causes rifts within the community. Viewing the office staff as an integral part of the school's team rather than a department that sits on a separate rung of an imaginary ladder of status is key when creating a workplace that nurtures cooperation, collaboration, and consideration. When all members of a school's team understand that they play equally important roles in the educational process, then the community will run more smoothly and effectively.

BUILD COMMUNITY: DO NOT STAND ALONE

In the teaching profession, one of the greatest rewards is the positive reinforcement teachers receive through the praise and affirmation of others. The temptation for new teachers may be to stand alone when receiving such praise, when in reality, practicing humility and appreciating those who helped contribute to your success as a teacher will take you much further in this profession. One of my students once commented that I should be glad that a coworker of mine did not share the same high standards that I possessed as a teacher because this would make me look better as a teacher. I quickly replied that this was truly not the case; bringing someone else down does not contribute to your success as a teacher, and it is better to work in a community of excellence than to stand alone. It is normal to encounter situations in schools in which it is difficult to work with certain individuals, and in these cases, it is best to complete your work with minimal interaction with these particular people. Negative energy and conflict should be avoided as much as possible in any workplace. However, teachers can usually find gems that surface in their school communities who are well regarded for their efficient work and their kind, collegial nature, and it is with these individuals that strong working relationships should be cultivated.

At the end of one of our spring semesters, a dedicated colleague with whom I had once worked came to address the graduating class of student teachers at our university. He is a very well-respected and successful English teacher who also headed the English Department at the high school. One of the greatest lessons that he shared with the student teachers was that success, as a department and as a school, is only achieved *together.* He went on to describe the English Department as a community sharing everything—tests, quizzes, and lessons were all communal property. He pointed out that although each member has different skills and strengths, each brings something to the table that adds to the meal. He reminded the student teachers that in education, we all share a single purpose, and so we should work together to achieve that goal. Cooperation, collaboration, and consideration are all required for the success of that purpose. In the same way, teachers should learn to include staff members in these communal efforts, working in an environment of mutual respect and understanding. My colleague's culminating words still resonate in my meditations as a teacher: "If you try to stand alone, you will be like a coal pulled from a fire, slowly growing cold and lifeless."

SURROUND YOURSELF WITH GOOD PEOPLE WHENEVER YOU CAN

The best advice that my first principal gave me was to surround myself with good people. Let this thought echo in your head as you meet new staff members and colleagues each year and work to grow friendships and working relationships. Build a network of friends and colleagues with these supportive staff members and exceptional classroom teachers, and whenever given the opportunity to work with them, take it. Partner with them on school committees, design integrated lessons, collaborate with them in action research projects, or work with them to locate resources for your class. Through working with these fine individuals and maintaining friendships with them, while enjoying their company and your time spent together, you will also find that their wisdom, knowledge, and standards for excellence are contagious and will energize you and motivate you to do better. Good teachers are constantly reflecting, changing, and growing. Although it is often difficult to keep up the stamina to be a good teacher in a profession in which bureaucracy and negativity can get the best of you, surrounding yourself with people who rise above this and strive to excel in all that they do is empowering and refreshing.

MAKE AND MAINTAIN TEACHER FRIENDS

One of the most satisfying stages of teacher development comes when new teachers realize that they have "teacher friends." It is a joy to find others in the teaching profession whom one can confide in, commiserate with, and console. A network of collegial support is vital to teachers for sharing their emotional and professional concerns. Nevertheless, it is also important to maintain boundaries and to strike a balance with colleagues so that one's professional time is not overwhelmingly consumed by these new associates. Spending too much time talking to other teachers during a planning period or during other times when work needs to be completed is not an effective way to manage time as a teacher. Given this precaution, when maintained correctly, relationships with teacher friends are essential resources for teachers.

Having a teacher friend in the same subject or grade level is ideal for sharing both emotional and specific pedagogical support. But if such collegial relationships cannot be found in one's own grade level or subject area, this should not deter teachers from cultivating these valuable relationships. Although subject-specific teaching methods or classroom management strategies may have to be modified a bit, the emotional and professional support shared with these colleagues will become priceless.

Teacher friends are definitely needed to provide emotional support. It is helpful to have a colleague who can identify with the details of your school's community and can empathize and offer a fresh perspective on any work situation. If it is possible to carpool with a fellow teacher, this will become a treasured time set aside and guarded each day to invest in a collegial relationship. This time can be used to vent and to resolve work issues in the car, while also getting to know a colleague more personally. New teachers should be careful to carpool with colleagues who match their personalities or who are positively invested in teaching. Carpooling with someone who is burned out on teaching can be detrimental for a new teacher, whereas carpooling with a colleague who can offer advice and support is comforting and encouraging. I always say that the best year of my teaching, as well as the best year of my marriage, was the year that I carpooled with one of my colleagues. I was comforted, refreshed, and energized for another day of work from our simple conversation in the car, and my husband was happy to see me a little more relaxed and decompressed after my ride home. The emotional support that fellow teachers can offer is extremely valuable, so any efforts made to plug into these relationships is highly recommended.

In my initial years of teaching, I also learned many pedagogical and managerial tips from teacher friends who did not teach the same content or grade level as I did. My friend from the English Department

shared her substitute letter and other practical management strategies with me (see Resources for an example substitute letter), and
she was also the carpool partner whom I shared many emotional
meltdowns with after school. Another teacher friend who taught
French shared her creative culture projects with me, and I was able
to modify them so that the lessons used the Spanish language
instead of French. This teacher also shared her participation point
system with me, and I continue to share it with my student teachers
today (see Chapter 3). At the elementary level, teachers who do not
teach the same grade level can share classroom management
strategies, such as methods for taking lunch count quickly. It is also
helpful to collaborate with those who teach different grade levels so
that you know what development levels your students are coming
from, or which levels you are preparing them for in the future. So,
teacher friends who do not teach the same content area or grade
level can still offer many practical teaching tips.

BE PURPOSEFUL ABOUT SPENDING TIME WITH YOUR FAVORITE COLLEAGUES

Once you have identified some valuable colleagues, making intentional efforts to spend time with them at least once every two weeks
is important. At one of the high schools where I worked, I met
regularly with a small group of teachers who were also working
mothers. During one of our planning periods, someone ran to the
local sandwich and coffee shops and brought back delicious sand-
wiches and specialty coffee drinks. The time was a real treat for
everyone, with rich conversation, wonderful support, and delicious
food. At the elementary level, our grade level met each Friday after
school for pizza and sodas. The preparation was simple, and the
time was found to be most valuable. Teachers need other teachers
to help renew and rejuvenate one another in this way.

If the school year is to be viewed like a marathon, then reaching
each mile marker throughout the year should be celebrated. Attend
happy hours or have coffee at the end of the week with colleagues,
have holiday parties with your fellow teachers, and find other creative ways to encourage one another and celebrate milestones
throughout the year with colleagues. When I taught at the elementary school level, the teachers all planned to celebrate the end of the

school year with some fun activity, like playing laser tag together. It was hilarious to see them all sweating in their laser tag gear and releasing a year's worth of stress and anxiety through this cardio-aerobic activity. When I was a secondary teacher, it became a weekly ritual for me to join one or more of my colleagues for a coffee date at the end of the week to celebrate another week under my belt as a new teacher. This time gave me the opportunity to get to know my colleagues on a more personal level, and also to rejoice with others in my profession about my triumphs in teaching.

EAT IN THE LUNCHROOM AND LEARN FROM YOUR COLLEAGUES

In my early years of teaching, I found that it was easy to remain isolated in my classroom working through lunch. I always felt that there was more to do and that I was always behind: I was in survival mode. According to research (Larabee, 2000; Rogers & Babinski, 2002; Schlichte, Yssel, & Merbler, 2005), isolation is one of the top concerns of a beginning teacher. As a new teacher, I found that it was especially easy to work through lunch with makeup exams and regular lunch meetings with students to help them make up their work and receive extra help. This was a mistake. Being collegial is a discipline; it is easy to become isolated and inactive in the community, especially as a new teacher. But this is not a wise practice. Reserve one specific day to help students during lunch, but do not give them every day. Eat in the lunchroom as much as possible during your first years on the job. This is where you will learn the parts of the school community, culture, and procedures that are not found in any handbook.

During my first year teaching high school, I learned a lot about the school's culture and traditions while talking to my colleagues in the lunchroom. I specifically remember learning about the annual Senior Service Day, and the ramifications of this day on teaching. The premise for this event was that senior students could be auctioned off to complete service in some way, but the seniors were not being treated properly so the event was discontinued the year after I began teaching. However, the point of this example is that I did not know about the inside culture of Senior Service Day and how to plan accordingly in my classroom for this particular day until I had engaged in a conversation in the faculty lunchroom. This type of information, in addition to the school's history and background information concerning school or community politics, is valuable to know and can all be learned in the lunchroom. This insider knowledge is helpful to new teachers as they plan their lessons and classroom activities. Understanding how the school's culture, traditions, and special activities affect classroom learning and instruction is critical for the success of new teachers.

TALK TO PEOPLE TO UNCOVER HIDDEN RESOURCES

Once teachers begin to talk to those around them, they will begin to uncover the hidden resources found in their schools. When I was a new teacher at the elementary level, I noticed that there was a staff person who was always at the photocopy machine. I assumed that she was a resource aide, but one day I initiated a conversation with her and discovered that she was hired to help all the teachers with their photocopying and laminating. Later, I found the area where teachers could submit their photocopy requests and laminating projects, and she would complete all these tasks for us. It is amazing when teachers calculate the numbers of hours that can be spent on these clerical tasks. It was like finding a precious gem when I uncovered this helpful resource from simply talking to someone by the photocopy machine.

Similarly, when new teachers first begin their jobs, it is difficult to learn about all the resources available to them because they are already overwhelmed with district orientations that deal with health benefits and other procedures, not to mention learning the entire curriculum to prepare their lessons. I know that I felt this way when I began teaching first grade. I was fortunate because the staff at the elementary school that I worked at was extremely warm and friendly, and the reading specialist asked me early on if I would like her to come in to present a guest lesson during the initial weeks of school. Observing her work with my first graders was helpful to me, both emotionally and professionally. In addition, the program coordinator visited my class and demonstrated other teaching strategies that she encouraged me to integrate into my lessons. Within my own school were a plethora of valuable resources that I might not have discovered on my own as a new teacher. But talking to the other staff members and being open to their help led me to incredible, free resources that helped me to survive and thrive in my early years in teaching.

PRACTICE RANDOM ACTS OF KINDNESS

Due to the nature of our hectic schedules in schools, we are often so driven by our work that personal greetings and conversations are eliminated from our interactions with our coworkers. In teaching, it is easy to talk about our work and our students, moving on to complete the procedural tasks on our list. However, taking time once in a while to get to know those whom we work with and to greet them personally builds a sense of community and helps teachers' overall enthusiasm and production in schools. Practicing random acts of kindness at our schools is a valuable tip that I learned early on in my teaching career that helped me to build bridges and to express my appreciation for those who helped make my job a little easier.

A key life lesson that my dear grandmother taught me through example when I was young comes to mind to model this lesson. My grandmother moved to the United States from South Korea, and she did not speak much English besides "Nobody home," which was followed by the hanging up of our home telephone. However, when the man who cleaned our pool came to our house regularly, Grandma would go outside each time to greet him with a smile, a cold drink, and a snack. She told me that we need to show people that we appreciate them, especially those who can easily be forgotten, like the pool man. As a teacher, I applied this principle to my work, recognizing the office and custodial staff as those whom I wanted to affirm in some special way for their work. In teaching, I followed Grandma's example and frequently left treats and thank-you notes for the custodial staff. Although teachers are fortunate to interact and receive positive feedback from students and others, the nightly custodial staff arrive after school hours to clean our rooms and do not have these benefits. Showing them our appreciation for their work affirms them, which I believe fuels their strong work ethic. Their excellence, in turn, contributes to the teacher's excellence.

In addition, simple and random expressions of gratitude and appreciation contribute to a positive working environment. When I saw the custodial staff after school, they would stop to greet me and share a friendly conversation. These personal connections and positive working relationships helped contribute to my success as a teacher, because through this network of staff members, special requests and accommodations were quickly and eagerly fulfilled. Whenever I needed help moving something to my room, an extra large trashcan for special activities, or extra cleaning after special activities, the staff would gladly and graciously help me.

Once when I served as the cheerleading advisor of our local high school, we decided to have a rummage sale to help the cheerleaders raise funds for their activities. The families and the public all wanted to donate large items for the rummage sale, but we did not know how we were going to transport the larger items to the school for our event. I was sharing this challenge with one member of our custodial staff, and he immediately offered to drive his truck around town with me on his day off to pick up the items and then deliver them to the school. This is one example of how the communal efforts of both teachers and staff can accomplish good things that benefit the students and the school.

IT'S ALL WHO YOU KNOW

To this day, I return to the schools in which I taught and greet the custodial staff, the cafeteria workers, the security, and the office staff with hugs and smiles. These are the valuable network of friends and colleagues that I have met and maintained in the teaching profession. I am a firm believer that you reap what you sow. When beginning teachers enter the teaching profession, it can be extremely intimidating to enter the culture of a new school wanting desperately to succeed as a new teacher. Often, teaching is viewed as an isolating profession, but in my experience as a teacher and teacher educator, I believe that being or feeling isolated as a beginning teacher is a choice. Teachers can choose to remain in their classrooms and disregard the support and the resources available outside in their school's community, or they can choose to embrace that support by reaching out and learning from others. Teachers have the choice to stand alone or to be a part of a team. Another life lesson learned here is that making connections and building bridges are extremely valuable. As I have always taught my students, a key lesson in their professional and personal lives is "It's all who you know."

CONCLUSION

Teaching requires a team effort. A teacher's success lies not only in the ability to teach well but also in the ability to be a team player. This involves communicating and cooperating with all those who are involved in the educational enterprise. A school's staff consists of a number of the people with whom a teacher must work collaboratively throughout the school year. Building bridges with these people and supporting them in their work will help them to reciprocate the same efforts to make teaching easier for all involved. Cooperation, collaboration, and consideration are all required for success in the teaching profession. When teachers choose to remain isolated in their classrooms and fail to appreciate, affirm, and acknowledge others at their school sites, they are quickly left burned out and disheartened by the rigor of teaching. Success in teaching is not achieved by standing alone.

❧ Practical Tips ❧

- Acknowledge the staff as part of the team.
- Build community: Do not stand alone.
- Surround yourself with good people whenever you can.
- Make and maintain teacher friends.
- Be purposeful about spending time with your favorite colleagues.
- Eat in the lunchroom and learn from your colleagues.
- Talk to people to uncover hidden resources.
- Practice random acts of kindness.
- Build networks within your school's community because, in the end, it's all about who you know.

C H A P T E R   N I N E

Parents and Teachers

We're on the Same Team

Teamwork is the ability to work together toward a common vision. The ability to direct individual accomplishments toward organizational objectives. It is the fuel that allows common people to attain uncommon results.

—Andrew Carnegie

A review of the research literature that deals with beginning teacher concerns reveals that communicating with parents is commonly cited as one of the top concerns of new teachers (Gordon, 1991; Meister & Melnick, 2003; Veenman, 1984). This concern may stem mainly from the uneasiness or tension that teachers encounter in parent-teacher confrontations. The conflict that needs to be resolved is typically a result of the incongruence found when comparing the teacher's perspective of the situation, the parents' understanding of the student's experience, and the student's actual experience. The tension that results from trying to understand each party's perspective leads to the commonly cited concern of beginning teachers in communicating with parents. In the end, however, teachers, parents, and students should come to the understanding that all parties involved are on the same team, and the goal for students is one and the same—for them to succeed. To adopt this perspective, a mutual trust should be established among all parties so that the genuine interest in the student's success lies at the forefront of the team's efforts during their brief time of working together. So, before teachers, parents, and students become angry and react impulsively regarding any issue that may arise, we should all stop to acquire the facts of any given situation and then harness together all the resources available to improve the learning outcomes for the student. How can we promote this sense of trust and partnership in education? In this chapter, suggestions on how to develop the teamwork approach to education are offered so that parents and teachers can work together to help students succeed.

COMMUNICATE REGULARLY AND CLEARLY WITH THE FRONT LINE OF RESOURCES

Although a teacher's day is filled from beginning to end with teaching and clerical responsibilities, it is imperative that teachers communicate openly and regularly with parents, other teachers, and even coaches regarding the progress of students, especially those who are at-risk or struggling in their academics. It is easy for teachers to push this task aside or leave it as a last resort, but connecting with these people is a frontline source for attacking a problem or addressing a student need. Opening the lines of communication at the beginning of the school year through letters from parents and students requesting information about the student's background and clarifying expectations (as suggested in Chapter 1 of this text) helps teachers to understand the student's academic history, to be aware of the parents' concerns, and to identify the student's strengths and weaknesses. In addition, teachers should make efforts to collaborate with other teachers and coaches, and these efforts should be communicated to parents. Former and current teachers of a student may offer pedagogical strategies that have proven to be effective or ineffective with the student, and coaches can serve as a motivating and supportive resource for the student. Parents can make known to the students that all who are involved in their education are communicating regularly, and as a result, expectations are made clear to the student from all angles. If parents, teachers, and coaches work together, motivational and instructional strategies can be maximized for students. Using this front line of resources will prove to be valuable to teachers throughout the year as they observe and monitor student growth, and parents will appreciate the open communication and collaboration of all those who are invested in their child's education.

MAKE A MEMORABLE IMPRESSION ON PARENTS AT BACK TO SCHOOL NIGHT

Back to School Night may be the first time that teachers connect personally with some parents. Therefore, this initial meeting is an important event at which teachers should make special efforts to leave memorable impressions on their audience. Unfortunately, Back to School Night can be viewed as an evening filled with mundane, ordinary presentations that parents sit through to meet their child's teacher and learn what procedures are followed in the various classrooms. A typical presentation may involve a personal introduction of the teacher followed by the review of state standards and the syllabus or goals for the class. Imagine being the parents in this situation: After a long day of work, you rush to your child's school and frantically run to each class, only to attend presentations similar to those you have seen every year at the elementary level, or six periods of the same content applied in different contexts at the secondary level. However, by adding a few details to the overall presentation, teachers can make Back to School Night a memorable, positive, and different experience for their audience. The following list offers some easy and practical suggestions for Back to School Night:

1. Provide a small basket of mints or snacks for parents as they walk into your classroom. This small gesture of hospitality is appreciated and sets a nice welcoming message for your guests.

2. Play music as parents enter the classroom and also as they exit. This helps to avoid awkward moments of silence, and also adds a positive tone to the classroom.

3. Provide several sign-in sheets for the parents. If parents are lined up out the door to sign the sign-in sheet, they may miss some of the presentation. Invite the guests inside the classroom and then have several sign-in sheets rotating throughout the classroom to help avoid the bottleneck effect at the door.

4. Include the students in some way in your presentation. Sometimes teachers can get caught up with explaining the rules and procedures in Back to School Night and forget to include the students somehow when covering the objectives or purposes of the class. Providing visuals of the students working, showcasing a piece of student work, or sharing personal stories from the beginning of the school year about the students brings a smile to the parents' faces and reminds everyone that our work is all being done for the students.

5. Ask for what you need. A creative way to share a teacher's wish list with parents is to have different items written on Post-it notes and then allowing parents to select the Post-it note that has the item that they believe is most feasible for them to provide. Parents then take the Post-it note home with them as a reminder to fulfill the teacher's wish. Examples for the Post-it notes include but are not limited to file folders, reams of paper, art supplies, science dissection kits, garden supplies for the class garden, and special reading books. Although elementary school teachers are typically the ones who are known to request a list of supplies to be brought in at the beginning of the year, secondary teachers should also be encouraged to ask for needed supplies. One social science teacher whom I knew constructed a wish list of items that was made available during Back to School Night. Included in the itemized list were art supplies for a map-making exercise. Soon, the teacher was supplied with storage bins filled with markers, colored pencils, and special paper. The teacher saved a tremendous amount of time and money by simply asking for donations. It only proves that the old saying is true, "You'll never know unless you ask," and usually in the world of teaching, we're better off than when we started.

6. Provide something visual in your presentation. It is true that a picture paints a thousand words, so rather than spending the whole time talking to all the parents about what you do as a teacher, show them by providing examples, or pictures of the students doing their work for your class. When my son was in the second grade, I attended his Back to School Night, and I was completely impressed with the presentation because it was so different from the many others that I had attended, so personal, and so memorable. After the teacher's personal introduction, she said that she and her students wanted to show the parents what they had been doing since the beginning of school. The teacher had taken pictures since the first day of school of classroom activities, the new jungle gym on the play yard, their computer time, their work with the PE teacher, and more. This short, entertaining PowerPoint slide presentation was set to the upbeat tune of "All Star" from the *Shrek* soundtrack. The presentation gave all the guests an idea of what had been accomplished in the first month of school and also gave the parents a sense of comfort and joy to know that their children were in such good hands. After the visual presentation, some quick announcements were made, but overall, I truly got a sense of what was going on in second grade from the PowerPoint presentation and the brief personal introduction of the teacher.

These special details will be sure to make Back to School Night memorable for your guests, and you will be the one who is remembered in the parents' minds when they return home to talk about the teachers whom they met.

DOCUMENT EVERYTHING!

It is important for teachers to document student behavior, achievement, and all methods of support and intervention that have been offered to students so that this information can be clearly communicated to parents and administrators should any concerns or inquiries arise. Saving parent e-mails, keeping a portfolio of student work, noting specific confrontations with students in a log, or telling another colleague or administrator what is going on early in the process of working with a special student are all important ways that teachers can document their efforts to help a student. This section describes some practical ways that teachers can document important information that will be helpful to them when working with parents.

Keep a Phone Log

Parent phone calls should be recorded in a notebook, whether or not parents were successfully contacted or if the attempt was simply made. The phone log could resemble the following format:

Date	Time	Student	Number called	Successful (S) or Unsuccessful (U)	Concern/Action Taken
3–29–07	2:45 p.m.	John Boy	xxx-xxxx	U	Left message on voice-mail regarding missing assignments
3–29–07	2:50 p.m.	Jane Girl	xxx-xxxx	S	Mother answered; discussed poor test scores and missing assignments

Teachers may choose to document parent phone calls in other ways, like writing them on individual student information cards rather than in a phone log. Although the particular format used is not important, the information that is recorded (as suggested above) is vital. These pieces of evidence are concrete data that teachers can refer to when discussing a student's case with parents, administrators, or resource staff.

Use Index Cards to Document Parent Contacts and Student Situations

Another practical method of documenting student information and parent contacts is to have an index card written out for each student that lists the parent contact information and any special needs of the student that the parent has brought to your attention. If disciplinary actions were carried out or if parent communication has been made, the teacher can note these actions, along with their corresponding dates, on the student's index card. The card can be conveniently filed in a box and easily carried along to any conference. When disciplinary actions have been taken, it is also recommended that the student sign on the line of the card where the episode was documented. This assures that the student has acknowledged the situation and the consequence. Documenting student situations and parent contacts in this simple yet practical way will prove to be valuable and helpful to teachers as they communicate with parents.

Keep a Portfolio of the Students' Work

By collecting student work in a portfolio throughout the year, teachers can have a folder of data accessible to them that presents evidence of students' efforts and achievements in class. I recall a personal experience when a student's portfolio was extremely helpful to me. I had to explain a high school student's grade to her father, who was livid because his daughter was failing my Spanish class. I had brought a portfolio of the student's work to this particular conference that included tests and quizzes of scores ranging from D's to F's. My gradebook also evidenced that the student had not turned in her homework consistently throughout the semester. The father was left speechless because the evidence that I had gathered, collected, and presented indicated that the student had failed to produce the work for a passing grade. It was an unfortunate episode, but having documented the appropriate items, I felt confident as I displayed the data to prove to the parent that I did not have a personal vendetta against his daughter; rather, it was her choice not to produce the work. In this case, the documentation served as concrete evidence that could not be disputed and that placed the responsibility back upon the student.

At every level of education, parents want to see what has been done or what is being done for their children. Keeping and maintaining a system that documents student records helps teachers show and explain to parents how their students are performing in class, as well as what efforts have been made to support them in their learning.

E-MAIL PROMPTLY AND CAREFULLY

With the rise of technological inventions like e-mail, it has become easier to access people daily, informally, and more quickly. This has added greater expectations for teachers in many areas to respond to parents more quickly and more frequently regarding their students' progress. Because the expectation of e-mail is to receive a response right away, teachers should do their best to respond promptly, even if it is just a brief note to let the parents know that the teacher has heard from them and will get back to them with more detailed information later. The teacher failing to acknowledge the parent's note may increase the parent's frustrations, so it is recommended that the teacher reply to the parent with a quick response that simply acknowledges the parent's e-mail:

> Dear Mr./Mrs./Ms. _____,
>
> I have received your e-mail and appreciate that you have brought these concerns to my attention. I would like to dedicate the time that your response merits, but am presently tied up all day with classes and meetings. Your e-mail is important to me, so I will do my best to respond promptly. Thank you for your patience.

In addition, the tone and timing of one's e-mail should be carefully considered. In terms of parent e-mail, the parents may not have considered all the circumstances of a situation, and they may have trusted their child's perspective of a situation to be the truth. In defending their child, the parents' e-mail may take a negative or hostile tone, so teachers should take these factors into consideration. Words chosen in e-mail can take on a tone that is much stronger than the writer intended, so readers should be careful to consider the diction used in this mode of communication. In this same way, teachers should be cautious in how they choose their words when responding to e-mail, and they should not reply to e-mail when they are angry. Both teachers and parents should take the time to consider carefully all aspects of a given situation before flippantly composing and sending e-mail.

The example below presents an appropriate and inappropriate response to an angry parent's e-mail:

> *Angry Parent:* I have just looked at my son's quarter grades that have been posted on your Web site, and there are some zeros. My son is an "A" student, and I cannot believe that I was not aware of these missing assignments earlier. I do not understand why I was not notified of this and would think that this would raise a red flag immediately. Are these over-sights on your part, or has he really not been doing his work??? This is not like him to not turn in assignments. He cannot afford to get anything lower than an A.

> ✗ *Inappropriate Response:* I have sent several notes home about _____'s missing assignments, but you obviously have not received them. The grades are updated each week online for our class, so you could check at the end of each week to see what particular assignment your son was missing. It is not too late for him to improve his grade, but he needs to be more responsible about completing his assignments for the class.

> ✓ *Appropriate Response:* I understand your concern about your son's missing assignments and would like to discuss possible strategies to help motivate him to com-plete his work. Several notes about missing assignments have been sent home, but no response was received. In addition, grades have been updated online each week so that parents can see what has or has not been com-pleted throughout the quarter. I think it would be help-ful to meet after school one day with (student's name) so that we could review what assignments are missing together and see how we could work together to help support him in the future. Please let me know the best dates and times that you are available. Thank you.

From the examples above, it is clear that syntax and diction can highly influence the tone that is portrayed in e-mail. For instance, it is evident that "you" statements should be avoided so as to reduce the possibility of sounding accusatory or negative. In addition, to set a positive or empathetic tone, it is best for teachers to begin their response by acknowledging the parent's concern and making clear that they, too, would like to resolve the issue and work together to find a solution. Placing the focus back on the students and having them accept the responsibility to make changes is also important. When teachers and parents are the only ones involved in discussions, the students tend to be left out of the learning process. Paying close attention to these details will help teachers and parents to communicate more clearly with one another.

It is also good practice to have someone else read an e-mail before sending it to assure that no offense is taken from the words that were chosen. For example, in my work with preparing student teachers for the teaching profession, we dedicate one seminar to an e-mail response exercise in which the student teachers respond to real parent e-mail that my colleagues have received. All identifying information is deleted from the e-mail, and student teachers are given the background information of the student's situation. Each group of student teachers is given an e-mail to which they must articulate a response to share with the class. After reading the responses, the writers of the e-mails are given feedback on their choice of words. In the end, the student teachers understand how their words can portray a negative or demeaning tone. Both beginning and veteran teachers should also take note of the lesson learned from this exercise and be careful in the choice of words used in e-mail.

Some special student cases are also better resolved with a meeting rather than through written words. Teachers should assess student situations accordingly and be cautious in how they use e-mail as a form of parent communication. Generally, quick updates and responses to simple questions that parents may have regarding clarification of student assignments or class updates can be answered through e-mail, but explanations of special student disciplinary cases or patterns of incomplete or substandard work are best resolved through telephone calls or conferences. Although e-mail is a convenience for many in current times, it should not be considered the only method of communication between teachers and parents. Cautions should be taken so that when e-mail is used, it can be used effectively and not cause more hurt feelings and misunderstandings.

BE SENSITIVE

When teachers become heavily involved in their own work and so focused on their teaching practices, they can fall into the trap of assuming that those around them come from a similar upbringing, have the same knowledge base about the teaching and learning process, and draw upon the same resources. Being so focused on a specific grade level or subject matter, teachers can slip into the mind-set that if the subject matter or grade level is easy for them, then it should be easy for everyone. It is puzzling and often frustrating for beginning teachers to understand why certain students do not grasp a particular learning concept or skill. The beginning teacher literature claims that beginning teachers are more focused on how they are doing, whereas expert teachers focus more on how the students are doing (Woolfolk, 2004). Given these findings, beginning teachers should make efforts to be careful to take into account that students must comply with a more stringent set of academic standards than ever before, and that parental support, language barriers, and cultural differences all serve as other variables that factor into the learning process.

Research Student Backgrounds and Become Knowledgeable About Cultures That Are Different From Your Own

It is helpful for teachers to be aware of the various socioeconomic, cultural, and family dynamics represented in today's classrooms. New teachers should research the student populations and communities that they are working with in their schools. By comparing these findings with their own personal backgrounds, teachers can identify the differences between themselves and their students and achieve cultural competencies in areas that were foreign to them. For instance, some teachers may not be accustomed to dealing with populations who are living in poverty, families of minority backgrounds, or same-sex parents. This information may be noted in students' cumulative folders or can be revealed by talking to the students, parents, or counselors.

One of my colleagues once worked with a group of students who were enrolled in a class called "Opportunity." It was the last "opportunity" for these students to stay in high school and work toward credits for graduation. The class was composed of a group of at-risk teenagers who had a long history of violations in and outside of school, earned poor grades, and represented minority groups. At the beginning of the school year, before addressing the curriculum, my colleague spent a great deal of time researching the students' cumulative folders and trying to understand their personal backgrounds. A personal and positive rapport with the students was established before focusing on the subject matter. Understanding the students and their cultures helped the teacher to gain the students' respect and their attention. Through efforts like these, a positive academic learning experience can be established and made accessible to all students.

Offer Parents the Resources Necessary to Help Their Students

Being sensitive to understanding what resources students have outside of school is extremely helpful when trying to support student learning. Having worked with my own sons on their language arts homework at the primary level, I can see how students whose parents are English-language learners are at a severe disadvantage when completing worksheets. If they do not understand or cannot read the directions or do not have the cultural knowledge to help the students with the homework, then these students do not have these resources to assist them in learning. In addition, working or single parents may not have or may not extend the resource of time or energy to students, so these special circumstances may leave these students at a disadvantage with both their daily homework and more extensive projects. Given these dilemmas, it is greatly appreciated when teachers can offer parents practical suggestions on how to help their students. Often, the parents simply do not know all the teaching tips and pedagogical knowledge to help their child improve their academic skills.

When my son was in kindergarten, his teacher invited a small group of parents in after school and shared several phonemic awareness strategies with them to help them work with their sons and daughters. The teacher also made small phonemic awareness exercise books for the students to work on in the car and at home. Some parents were English-language learners and were formally learning English sounds for the first time so that they could help support their children's language development at home. The parents greatly appreciated these suggestions, and together they all worked as a team to lay a foundation for reading for the students. Being sensitive to the diverse backgrounds of students and helping equip parents with the resources needed to support their students in education are useful ways that teachers can partner with parents to maximize learning in their classrooms.

CONCLUSION

One of the greatest rewards in teaching is to see the students learn and succeed and to know that you, as a teacher, played a pivotal role in that process. More often than not, that role involves more than simply teaching the subject matter. The role of teacher involves identifying obstacles in the student's learning, uncovering resources, partnering with parents and other teachers or coaches, and being sensitive to the student's special circumstances. Teaching is a process that involves many players, and when these players all unite as a team to attain the same goal, the learning and success of a child are inevitable.

⮞ Practical Tips ⮜

- Acknowledge that parents and teachers are on the same team.
- Communicate regularly and clearly with the front line of resources (i.e., parents, other teachers, and coaches).
- Make a memorable impression on parents at Back to School Night.
- Document everything!
- Keep a phone log.
- Use index cards to document parent contacts and student situations.
- Keep a portfolio of the students' work.
- E-mail promptly and carefully.
- Be sensitive.
- Research student backgrounds and become knowledgeable about cultures that are different from your own.
- Offer parents the resources necessary to help their students.

CHAPTER TEN

Participate in the Profession

No calling in society is more demanding than teaching; no calling in our society is more selfless than teaching; and no calling is more central to the vitality of a democracy than teaching.

—Roger Mudd

The teaching profession offers a great deal of autonomy because teachers are left in their classrooms to make their own decisions as they plan and carry out each day's activities. In some respects, the teaching culture is slowly changing in this area, with more collaborative efforts being made among teachers of similar grade levels or departments to meet regularly to discuss curriculum, assessments, and evaluations. However, generally speaking, teachers tend to work independently. To some, this independence is an advantage, whereas to others, it can become a detriment. Although it may be easy to work alone and remain in one's classroom without interacting with colleagues during any given day, it is important for teachers to cultivate collegial relationships, participate in the profession of teaching, and invest in a professional learning community. Engaging in collegial interactions and contributing to the educational community are what distinguish a person who is a teacher from one who is a teaching professional. It is a reasonable expectation for new teachers to begin participating in teaching communities at their own school sites or within their district. This might entail team teaching or partnering with colleagues when mapping out learning units for the year, meeting, and discussing curriculum and course outcomes with teachers from other schools in the district or even attending teaching workshops within the district. As new teachers move past the challenging first years and become more confident in their teaching, they will begin to seek out more opportunities to learn, grow, and make contributions to their professional community. Teaching is not just an act that goes on in the classroom, but it is a profession and involves interacting with other professionals and becoming involved in the wider issues that affect the teaching community. This chapter offers suggestions on how beginning teachers can participate in the teaching profession and also describes the great values found in doing so.

SPEND PROFESSIONAL DEVELOPMENT DAYS LEARNING FROM ONE ANOTHER

In most school districts, a number of pupil-free days are set aside each year for professional development. Although the intention of these days is for teachers to add tools to their teaching repertoire or to reflect on their teaching with a new perspective derived from a workshop, teachers typically view these days as a time to catch up on grading papers or as precious time that is spent away from their classrooms. Often, an outside speaker is invited to present the latest trends or innovations in teaching, and although this can be helpful, some of the most valuable speakers for these professional development days can be found right within our schools. The most memorable and valuable professional development days for me at the elementary, secondary, and even college levels of teaching have been when my colleagues have presented the workshops and shared their teaching practices.

From my experience in education, I have found that teachers learn best from other teachers. They appreciate and are open to the words and wisdom of other colleagues who have worked in the trenches and have come out triumphant. Being in departmentalized school settings, it is rare for teachers to have the opportunity to hear about each other's work and best practices. Therefore, if a whole day has been set aside to inspire teachers to develop professionally, it is highly recommended that this time be used for teachers to learn from one another.

At the elementary level, I remember attending several break-out sessions in which my colleagues who specialized in math instruction presented hands-on workshops of how they taught various math lessons using the newly adopted math curriculum. Other teachers also presented their ideas about language arts instruction, and their sessions involved a "make it, take it" format in which participants created small storybooks or phonics-based projects. When teaching at the high school level, I presented a session about learning games that could be easily adapted to any subject area. This included a basketball learning game in which students earn a point for answering a question correctly and then can add up to four additional points to their team's score by shooting two additional baskets into the class trash can. (The details of this game are included in the Resources.) Throughout the year, teachers commented on how they were easily able to incorporate this activity into their classrooms right after the workshop. Sharing and learning practical teaching tips from colleagues are one way that teachers can grow in this profession.

I participated in our school's professional development day by presenting my teaching ideas when I was a fairly new teacher, and I point this out because beginning teachers often feel inadequate about sharing their work, their resources, or their talents with veteran teachers. Although beginning teachers often feel that they have nothing to offer their experienced colleagues, this is usually not true. New teachers can offer fresh, valuable ideas or many useful talents that can be helpful to their veteran colleagues. In cultivating collegial relationships, new teachers should remember that the relationship should be bidirectional, and it should not be assumed that the veteran teacher is the only one who is capable of offering ideas or resources. All teachers, new or experienced, can learn from one another.

PARTICIPATE AND NETWORK IN THE BROADER TEACHING COMMUNITY

Besides networking with colleagues and participating in one's own school community, it is important that teachers also participate in the broader teaching community. Teachers from different schools, districts, and states should come together to discuss teaching strategies, student outcomes, and the current state of education in our nation. Gathering together and engaging in professional discourse will help all teachers learn and grow more. The following section presents some practical ways that new teachers can participate in the broader teaching community.

JOIN PROFESSIONAL ORGANIZATIONS OR LISTSERVS

Many professional teacher organizations are available to offer a plethora of resources for teachers. Student teachers can begin by joining education honor societies while they are enrolled in their teacher preparation program, and then these memberships can continue on into their professional careers. Groups like Kappa Delta Pi, an international education honor society, have numerous resources on their Web site, extend teacher discounts, offer helpful teaching tips in their sponsored publications, and host annual conferences where teachers can gather together to learn from one another. New teachers should ask veteran teachers and administrators at their school sites about the professional organizations that have been most supportive in their teacher development. Colleagues who have been in the profession for a number of years may have participated in or found particular organizations to be most helpful. In addition, it is highly recommended that teachers ask their administrators which professional organizations the school or district might already be affiliated with so that group memberships may be obtained, or in some cases, the school district may even cover the teacher's membership. Many associations are based on the special interests of teachers. For instance, there are national kindergarten teacher groups, the National Council for Teachers of Mathematics, American Council for Teachers of Foreign Language, and various national and state teacher unions. A quick Internet search on your teaching specialty will yield multiple links to various organizations that offer endless resources and opportunities for professional development.

With the Internet at our fingertips, networking opportunities and support for teachers are readily available online. Many educational listservs have been created whose primary focus is to help K–12 teachers. By submitting one's e-mail address to a list-serv, the individual's e-mail will be added to the group's mailing list, and subsequent updates and announcements will automatically be sent from the organization. Educational listservs range from special interest groups that support integrating technology into teaching to K–12 teachers sharing their teaching ideas. The easiest way to find a listserv to join is to do an Internet search on "educational listserv" or again, ask your colleagues which list-servs they have joined and have found to be most helpful.

Besides joining listservs, teachers can find networking opportunities through education-related Web sites. In California, Web sites like www.edjoin.org post current teaching positions and recruiting fairs throughout the state on one Web site. Another useful resource for teachers has been www.teachers.net, which is an extensive Web site that brings together many teaching communities (student teachers, beginning teachers, elementary, secondary, special education, librarians, etc.) and presents free resources and discussion boards for members of these communities to post questions, seek advice, and offer solutions or support to their colleagues. There are numerous ways to connect with others in the teaching profession through avenues like these on the Internet.

ATTEND CONFERENCES AND BUILD PROFESSIONAL NETWORKS

Attending professional conferences is an excellent way to network and learn from teachers from different schools and districts throughout the state or the nation, as well as other representatives from the educational community. Teachers, university personnel, educational vendors, and book publishers all gather at these events to showcase their work or their products. Many schools encourage teachers to attend conferences and will cover or offset the costs for these professional development opportunities. It is important to stay current with the body of knowledge and the innovative teaching methodologies in one's field and to explore ways to develop professionally.

Professional conferences offer fresh ideas and teacher tools that can be incorporated immediately into one's teaching. Educators from all over the nation or from various parts of the world gather at these events to share their best practices. I have personally benefited from attending an educational technology conference sponsored by Computer Using Educators (CUE). Each year I bring back to my classroom at least one activity or tool that educators have shared during the conference sessions that can be quickly and practically integrated into my teaching. For instance, one year I learned about blogging, an online form of journaling, and discovered that by using www.blogger.com my student teachers could create their own free blog (short for "Web log"). My student teachers began to compose weekly blog entries that documented their reflections and experiences in their field placements. By clicking on to their blogs, I was able to read about their experiences, post my comments on their blogs, and review their development over time in their student teaching through these journal entries. One of my secondary English teaching candidates then went on to incorporate blogs in her own high school classroom by having students use this activity for their literary response journals. By learning about this free resource at a conference, I was able to assess my students' learning in a new, quick, and efficient manner, as well as share this innovation with a future teacher.

In addition to learning useful teaching tips, I have built a professional network at conferences by meeting other representatives from the educational community. At the exhibition halls, I have learned about new technological devices created to assist learning in the classroom, and after gathering business cards and making personal connections with the vendors, I have invited them to come to our school site to showcase their products. This is an excellent way to share these advancements in education with others at one's school site. Once administrators or other colleagues see the products, funding opportunities can be further discussed and explored, and more support can be built up to purchase the product for the school. Building professional relationships at conferences is also how I began the journey of writing this very book! After one of my conference presentations, an acquisitions editor approached me and took the time to discuss my book ideas and helped bring them to fruition. The networking opportunities found at conferences are extremely valuable, and this is a practical way for teachers to learn about teaching methods, tools, and other professional development opportunities.

PRESENT OR PUBLISH YOUR WORK

By sharing our work and learning from one another, teachers help each other to grow professionally. Teachers who have been recognized for their outstanding work should be encouraged to share their best practices with the larger educational community. This can be accomplished by presenting one's work at a professional conference or submitting articles to teacher magazines and education journals. After one of my exceptional student-teacher graduates began teaching, her principal and her school quickly recognized her innovative teaching talents. She felt encouraged to share her teaching ideas with teacher magazines like *Mailbox* and submitted proposals to present her work at national conferences. In just her third year of teaching, she was accepted to present at two national teacher conferences! If teachers are intimidated by sharing their practices in these ways, then they should attend conferences or read previous issues of selected journals to grasp a better understanding of the format of the presentations or articles. It was after watching many conference presentations that I felt motivated and confident enough to submit a proposal to share my work with others at future conferences. Presenting and publishing one's work adds to the knowledge base that educators can learn from and apply in their classrooms, and this will continually advance the methods used in our profession.

WRITE GRANTS

The teaching profession can also include members outside a school's realm. Teachers should partner with and tap into the resources offered by local and national funding agencies that wish to recognize good teaching and offer financial support for learning in classrooms. Web resources like www.infoed.org can be accessed to explore the multiple funding opportunities that are available for educators. Teachers often feel restricted when trying to implement their innovative teaching ideas due to lack of funding. However, teachers should explore and take advantage of the sources that are available to support classroom learning. For example, local businesses may sponsor particular classrooms or consolidate their efforts to make special grants available for teachers. In our local area, teachers apply for grants that have been created by a consortium of local business organizations that seek to recognize teachers for their exceptional teaching ideas and award them money to support them in their teaching. The recipients of the awards are recognized at a special banquet where members of the teaching profession gather to share and celebrate their work, and newspaper articles that showcase the teachers and their efforts follow the event. By taking up grant writing, teachers can partner with other sources both in and outside the educational community who will support their work and provide opportunities to further their development as teaching professionals.

ENGAGE IN ACTION RESEARCH

Teachers can take on the role of researchers in their own classrooms by engaging in action research. By making focused observations and documenting the data gathered from the work completed with students in their classrooms, teachers can answer research questions that address topics that range from effective versus ineffective teaching methods with particular student groups to how the time of day affects student achievement. Teachers can explore their research interests by using their classrooms as the setting for data collection. These experiments can then be shared with a broader research community at local or national conferences or in professional journals.

BE INFORMED AND VOTE

The longer I have participated in the teaching profession, the more new measures I have seen proposed in elections for education; budget, tenure, and restructuring schools are just a few issues that have been addressed that affect all teachers. Although I do not claim to be a political expert, I do believe that as a teaching professional, I must be informed and participate in the democratic process. By staying informed and casting their votes, teachers demonstrate that they are active participants in the teaching profession, a responsibility that often goes beyond and is affected by forces outside the confines of our classrooms.

CONCLUSION

To take advantage of all the resources that are available to them and to fulfill all their responsibilities as teaching professionals, teachers must discipline themselves to participate in the teaching community. This entails cultivating collegial relationships, networking with teachers from other schools and districts, partnering with others outside of teaching, and staying informed and current with the teaching practices and the body of knowledge in our field. To be a teacher is not simply to be active in a classroom; it also means that one is a member of a larger community of practicing professionals who can have a voice in the condition of today's schools and who can work together to improve them.

ಈ Practical Tips ೫

- Spend professional development days learning from one another.
- Participate and network in the broader teaching community.
- Join professional organizations or listservs.
- Attend conferences and build professional networks.
- Present or publish your work.
- Write grants.
- Engage in action research.
- Be informed and vote.

Conclusion

Success is a journey, not a destination.

—Author Unknown

Writing this book has taken me on a reflective journey as a teacher. I have looked back on my early years in teaching and tried to identify the reasons that I defied all the statistics and continued to teach. Along the path of this journey, I have revisited the special people, the schools, the classrooms, and students who shaped me as a teacher and inspired me to continue teaching. I will be forever grateful to all these people whom I have worked alongside or served through teaching, and from whom I continue to learn valuable lessons and the practical tips that contribute to my longevity in this profession.

With such an alarming percentage of new teachers leaving the profession today, educators need to do all that we can to support and sustain beginning teachers with the practical information that is unwritten and untold in school cultures. Ingersoll and Smith (2003) found that 40%–50% of beginning teachers leave the profession after just 5 years. As a professional community of teachers, we can help retain more teachers by uplifting, encouraging, and supporting new teachers through our body of knowledge, especially the knowledge that has been learned through our personal experiences, knowledge that has been left out of our formal education. Beginning teachers should not be left alone to figure out how to succeed in this profession. Instead, they should have access to free resources and valuable insider knowledge that will help them hit the ground running. It is my hope that the practical insights provided in this book will help new teachers to do just that—to have some insider information that will empower them and inspire them as they begin teaching.

The practical tips I provided in this book do not come simply from my observations of others' work: I applied most of these tips in my own classrooms and continue to use them. From being careful not to let my first impressions limit the learning potential of my students or the opportunities I could have with people I meet (Chapter 1) to learning how to manage my time effectively as a working mother (Chapter 2), this book comprises helpful life skills that I have found to be valuable both inside and outside the classroom.

After having identified the practical tips presented in this book, I was prompted to think of other similar times in life when we embark on a new journey, such as marriage or parenthood, and it seems as if those are also times when all those around us want to give us their personal advice for success. It is easy to feel bombarded and overwhelmed by all the essential bits of information that we should know. Through sharing these tips, my own struggles, and the life lessons learned as a beginning teacher, I hope that teachers out there who have just begun this journey, or perhaps are feeling burned out from it, might feel comforted in knowing that they are just "normal." New teachers should feel encouraged to know that others who have experienced the same challenges, often with even fewer resources, have survived and now thrive in the teaching profession. Similarly, for veteran teachers, my hope is that my words will uplift and energize them in a way that many of them need for pressing on with a renewed perspective on the great work that we do. As humans, I think that there is a part of all of us that needs to be reminded that the hardships we face, professionally and otherwise, are normal, and others like us have overcome them. As mentioned in Chapter 7, everyone needs a cheerleader in life. If this book has allowed me to be a cheerleader for teachers by giving them the tools needed to overcome some challenges, reminding them why they chose to dedicate their lives to this profession, and encouraging them to stick to it, then it has accomplished its purpose.

Resources

LOG KEEPER SHEET

TODAY'S DATE: _____ NAME OF LOG KEEPER _____

As Log Keeper you will **conscientiously** take **thorough notes** about

- the agenda,
- journal assignments,
- lecture notes (or offer to share your notes later),
- class activities and homework,
- absences and tardies.

If you were absent on the above date, please read the following and take handout(s) that are included behind this log assignment.

STUDENTS WHO WERE ABSENT TODAY: _____

STUDENTS WHO WERE TARDY TODAY: _____

AGENDA:

1.

2.

3.

4.

5.

WERE THERE HANDOUTS TODAY? Yes____ No ____ If so, how many? _____ (Be sure to include handouts behind this log assignment.)

SUMMARY (DETAILED ACCOUNT) of what went on in class today. Continue on additional paper if necessary. Be sure to include notes, handouts, and so forth, from the day's activities.

Note. Used with permission from Donna Fulgham, Language Arts Instructor, New Teacher Mentor, BTSA Trainer, National Board Certified Language Arts Teacher, Moorpark High School, Moorpark, California.

SUBSTITUTE LETTER

Date

Dear Substitute Teacher:

Thank you for taking my classes. My attendance book is on the lectern. My seating charts are in the attendance book. At the beginning of the period, please **mark my attendance book as well as the attached attendance sheet copies** that go to the office. For the attendance sheets, please write today's date along with "A" for absent, "T" for tardy. **Be sure to turn in these sheets to the office by the end of the day.** Only one class hall pass is available and rests on the whiteboard. I **rarely** let students go to the bathroom unless it is an emergency and **never** to their lockers so it shouldn't be an issue. **LESSON PLANS ARE ON THE TOP BOOK SHELF behind you** and agendas are on the board in order of periods.

My class schedule is as follows this year:

Period 1	7:30–8:26	English 1 Pre-AP	Freshmen
Period 2	8:31—9:31	(BTSA Support period)	
Period 3	9:36—10:32	(New Teacher Support)	
Period 4	10:37—11:33	English 4 AP	Seniors
LUNCH	11:33–12:13		
Period 5	12:13–1:14	English 4 AP	Seniors
Period 6	1:19–2:15	Prep	

During periods 2 and 3 (BTSA and New Teacher Support) please check in with Jane Doe regarding additional duties. She may have you sub in another room, assist her in the office, or undertake some other duty.

Sally is my Period 4 TA. She is very helpful and knows what is appropriate. She can take attendance to the office, run errands, and so forth. Please have her assist you as needed if she is present.

I doubt the need will arise, but if anyone gives you a difficult time, please write his or her name down for me with a brief description of the problem. I assure you I will address it as soon as I return.

Again, thank you for taking my classes. Have a great day.

Please note that the individual lesson plans are in separate folders on the bookshelf behind the podium. All required materials should be below each plan folder. Teacher textbooks are in the podium. Please DO NOT leave these out.

Note. Used with permission from Donna Fulgham, Language Arts Instructor, New Teacher Mentor, BTSA Trainer, National Board Certified Language Arts Teacher, Moorpark High School, Moorpark, California.

BASKETBALL

Materials

- A buzzer (from the "Taboo" game) or something your students can grab for, like a bean bag
- Some kind of small basketball (a miniature toy one or one that's homemade)
- Two wastebaskets or boxes
- Two students' desks that face each other

Basketball is an excellent game to play to review before a test or to check for understanding of a particular lesson. To set up the game, you need the above-listed materials arranged like this:

1. Place one wastebasket or box next to a wall. (The wall will serve as the backboard.)

2. Place two desks facing each other about 3 feet from that first wastebasket.

3. Place the buzzer in the middle of the two desks.

4. Place the second wastebasket in front of the two desks.

The whole set-up should look a little bit like this:

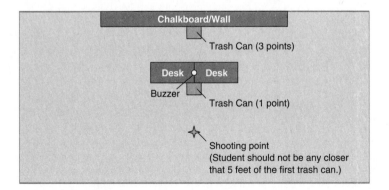

Divide the class into two teams. Have one member of each team come up to sit in their respective "hot seats." Ask them a question regarding the lesson being reviewed. The first person who buzzes in and responds correctly earns one point for the right answer and then gets to shoot the basketball twice. If the student makes the front basket, it is worth 1 point. A basket in the trash can situated next to the wall earns 3 points. So there is a total of 7 points possible for each participant. Homework passes or candy may be offered as rewards for the winning team.

References

Blaydes, J. (2003). *The educator's book of quotes.* Thousand Oaks, CA: Corwin Press.

Clark, R. (2004). *The excellent 11: Qualities teachers and parents use to motivate, inspire, and educate children.* New York: Hyperion.

Ginott, H. (1965). *Between parent and child.* New York: Macmillan.

Gordon, S. P. (1991). *How to help beginning teachers succeed.* Alexandria, VA: Association for Supervision and Curriculum. (ERIC Document Reproduction Service No. 341 166)

Ingersoll, R. M., & Smith, T. M. (2003, May). The wrong solution to the teacher shortage. *Educational Leadership, 60,* 30–33.

Jensen, E. (1995). *Brain-based learning and teaching.* Del Mar, CA: The Brain Store.

Jensen, E. (2000). Moving with the brain in mind. *Educational Leadership, 58,* 34–37.

Jensen, E. (2001). *Arts with the brain in mind.* Alexandria, VA: Association for Supervision and Curriculum Development.

Korthagen, F., Kessels, J., Koster, B., Lagerwerf, B., & Wubbels, T. (2001). *Linking practice and theory: The pedagogy of realistic teacher education.* Mahwah, NJ: Lawrence Erlbaum.

Larabee, D. F. (2000, May/June). On the nature of teaching and teacher education: Difficult practices that look easy. *Journal of Teacher Education, 51,* 228–233.

Maslow, A. (1968). *Toward a psychology of being.* Princeton, NJ: Van Nostrand.

Meister, D. G., & Melnick, S. A. (2003, Winter). National new teacher study. *Action in teacher education, 24,* 87–94.

Rogers, D. L., & Babinski, L. M. (2002). *From isolation to conversation: Supporting new teachers' development.* Albany, NY: SUNY Press.

Ryan, K. (1974). *Survival is not good enough: Overcoming the problems of beginning teachers* (Report No. AFT-Pap-15). Washington, DC: American Federation of Teachers. (ERIC Document Reproduction Service No. ED 090 200)

Schlichte, J., Yssel, N., & Merbler, J. (2005, Fall). Pathways to burnout: Case studies in teacher isolation and alienation. *Preventing School Failure, 50,* 35–40.

Sousa, D. (2001). *How the brain learns* (2nd ed.). Thousand Oaks, CA: Corwin Press.

Sylwester, R. (1995). *A celebration of neurons: An educator's guide to the brain.* Alexandria, VA: Association for Supervision and Curriculum Development.

Tate, M. L. (2003). *Worksheets don't grow dendrites: 20 instructional strategies that engage the brain.* Thousand Oaks, CA: Corwin Press.

Tate, M. L. (2004). *"Sit & get" won't grow dendrites: 20 professional strategies that engage the adult brain.* Thousand Oaks, CA: Corwin Press.

Veenman, S. (1984). Perceived problems of beginning teachers. *Review of Educational Research, 54,* 143–178.

Wolfe, P. (2001). *Brain matters: Translating research into classroom practice.* Alexandria, VA: Association for Supervision and Curriculum Development.

Woolfolk, A. (2004). *Educational psychology* (9th ed.). Boston: Allyn & Bacon.

Index